GUIDE TO THE FLIGHT REVIEW
For Pilots & Instructors

JASON BLAIR

NINTH EDITION

COMPLETE PREPARATION FOR ISSUING OR
TAKING A FLIGHT REVIEW INCLUDING BOTH
THE GROUND AND FLIGHT REQUIREMENTS

AVIATION SUPPLIES & ACADEMICS, INC.
NEWCASTLE, WASHINGTON

Guide to the Flight Review for Pilots and Instructors
Ninth Edition
by Jason Blair

Aviation Supplies & Academics, Inc.
7005 132nd Place SE
Newcastle, Washington 98059
asa@asa2fly.com | 425-235-1500 | asa2fly.com

Copyright © 2024 Aviation Supplies & Academics, Inc.
First edition published 1994. Ninth edition published 2024. Previously published as *Guide to the Biennial Flight Review*.

See the Reader Resources at asa2fly.com/oegbfr for additional information and updates relating to this book.

All rights reserved. No part of this publication may be reproduced, stored in a retrieval system, or transmitted in any form or by any means without the prior written permission of the copyright holder. While every precaution has been taken in the preparation of this book, the publisher and Jason Blair assume no responsibility for damages resulting from the use of the information contained herein.

None of the material in this book supersedes any operational documents or procedures issued by the Federal Aviation Administration, aircraft and avionics manufacturers, flight schools, or the operators of aircraft.

URLs appearing in this book are active at the time of publication, but site content may have since changed, moved, or been deleted.

ASA-OEG-BFR9
ISBN 978-1-64425-398-4

Additional formats available:
eBook EPUB   ISBN 978-1-64425-399-1
eBook PDF   ISBN 978-1-64425-400-4

Printed in the United States of America
2028   2027   2026   2025   2024   9   8   7   6   5   4   3   2   1

Library of Congress Cataloging-in-Publication Data
Names: Blair, Jason, author.
Title: Guide to the flight review for pilots & instructors : complete preparation for issuing or taking a flight review including both the ground and flight requirements / Jason Blair.
Description: Ninth edition. | Newcastle, Washington : Aviation Supplies & Academics, Inc., 2024. | First edition published 1994 as Guide to the biennial flight review by Jackie Spanitz.
Identifiers: LCCN 2024014565 (print) | LCCN 2024014566 (ebook) | ISBN 9781644253984 (trade paperback) | ISBN 9781644253991 (epub) | ISBN 9781644254004 (pdf)
Subjects: LCSH: United States. Federal Aviation Administration—Examinations—Study guides. | Airplanes—Piloting—Examinations—Study guides. | LCGFT: Study guides.
Classification: LCC TL710 .B557 2024 (print) | LCC TL710 (ebook) | DDC 629.132/52076—dc23/eng/20240415
LC record available at https://lccn.loc.gov/2024014565
LC ebook record available at https://lccn.loc.gov/2024014566

Contents

About the Author v

1 **Introduction**
   What is the Flight Review? 2
   Flight Review Candidates 2
   Requirements (14 CFR 61.56) 3
   Options for Completing the Flight Review 3
   Conduct of the Flight Review 4
   Reader Resources 5

2 **Q&A:**
   Candidate Information 8
   Instructor Information 14

3 **Ground Instruction Requirement**
   A. Privileges and Limitations 20
   B. Medical Qualifications and Considerations 22
   C. Currency Requirements 28
   D. Aircraft Certificates and Documents 30
   E. Aircraft Maintenance Requirements 32
   F. Weather 38
   G. Obtaining Weather Information 43
   H. sUAS Operations and the General Aviation Pilot 48
   I. Weather Reports, Forecasts and Charts 52
   J. Aerodynamics 57
   K. Weight and Balance 60
   L. Aircraft Performance 62
   M. Navigation 65
   N. Cross-Country Flying 67

O. Radio Communications 69
P. Federal Aviation Regulations Part 91 71
Q. Airspace 82
R. National Transportation Safety Board 99
S. Airport Operations 101
T. Runway Incursion Avoidance 106
U. Aviation Security 112
V. Aircraft and Engine Operations 114
W. System and Equipment Malfunctions 116
X. Airplane Instruments/Systems 121
Y. Human Factors 124
Review: Sample Written Exercise 133

4 Flight Instruction Requirement
Maneuvers Tables 138

Appendix 1 FAA Guidance Document: Conducting an
Effective Flight Review 141
Appendix 2 Flight Review Checklist 173
Appendix 3 Developing Personal Minimums 177
Appendix 4 FAA Over-the-Counter (OTC) Medications
Reference Guide 183

About the Author

Jason Blair is an active single- and multi-engine instructor and an FAA Designated Pilot Examiner (DPE) with over 6,000 hours total time, over 3,500 hours of instruction given, and more than 3,500 hours in aircraft as a DPE. In his role as an Examiner, he has issued more than 2,500 pilot certificates. Blair has worked for and continues to work with multiple aviation associations with his work focusing on pilot training and testing. His experience as a pilot goes back over 30 years, as an instructor spans over 20 years, and includes more than 100 makes and models of aircraft flown. Blair has written and continues to write for multiple aviation publications with a focus on training and safety.

In addition to ASA's Oral Exam Guide series, Blair is also the author of four books in ASA's Aviator's Field Guide series: *Buying an Airplane, Owning an Airplane, Tailwheel Flying,* and *Middle-Altitude Flying.*

Introduction 1

1 Introduction

What is the Flight Review?

This guide to the flight review (previously called "Biennial Flight Review" or BFR) is a comprehensive guide to prepare for taking or issuing a flight review. The flight review has been an FAA requirement since 1974 and was developed to curb pilot-related accidents. Although it has accomplished this objective, there is still room for improvement. A standard flight review should offer an effective learning experience that will further reduce pilot-related accidents. The FAA's guidance document reprinted in Appendix 3 provides some excellent and very specific recommendations on how to use the flight review in this capacity.

The flight review is not intended to be another checkride, but rather an assessment of the pilot's skills. The sole objective is to determine if the pilot is safe in the operations they usually conduct.

Again, the flight review is meant to determine your ability to handle the airplane safely and with good judgment. It is not meant to be like the checkride, but rather instructional. The maneuvers performed in the flight should reflect the pilot's experience and type of flying; the actions should be predictable to the instructor and conform to local procedures, with safety being the main concern. The flight review should be considered an opportunity. It could be performed annually, as recurrent or refresher training, or biennially, as required by 14 CFR §61.56.

Flight Review Candidates

14 CFR §61.56 states that every pilot must take a flight review every 24 calendar months. This means *every* pilot must take a flight review in order to maintain pilot-in-command (PIC) privileges.

Requirements (14 CFR 61.56)
The conduct of the flight review is at the discretion of the flight instructor, but the FAA does state minimum requirements necessary for the satisfactory completion:

- 1 hour of flight training and 1 hour of ground training
- A review of 14 CFR Part 91
- A review of those maneuvers and procedures necessary for the pilot to demonstrate the safe exercise of the privileges of the pilot certificate
- A logbook endorsement stating the satisfactory completion of the check

See 14 CFR §61.56, and Appendix 1 for the FAA's recommendations on content and best use of time during the flight review.

Options for Completing the Flight Review
With safety in mind, the flight review can be completed in a manner beneficial to the pilot:

- *A flight review with a flight instructor*

Everyone can use some dual flight periodically. This would be a prime opportunity to brush up on skills not frequently used. If flights normally take place at a nontowered airport, flight into a busier airport could increase proficiency in radio communications, and airspace. If straight and level is the normal attitude, some unusual attitudes and hood-work would be beneficial. If flights are normally conducted within the local area, a cross-country could be planned.

This is the suggested route to take for those that don't have the opportunity to fly as frequently as they might like—work off that rust! *See* Appendix 3 for the FAA's recommendations on how to conduct an effective flight review.

- *Upgrade your pilot or flight instructor certificate*

The FAA does not specify which aircraft a candidate must use for the flight review (however, this might change in the future). With this in mind, this would be a prime opportunity to get that instrument rating, sea rating, multi-engine rating, glider license, or helicopter license. Any checkride meets the requirements of a flight review, so the sky's the limit! The FAA also states the flight review requirements can be accomplished in combination with other recency requirements:

interpreted, this means candidates can become night current, instrument current, or tailwheel current (keep in mind that additional tasks will be added to meet both requirements).

This is the suggested route for those who are flying frequently, have little rust on their skills, and who are looking to expand their flying horizons. Again, safety is the main issue, and careful consideration should be taken before deciding which aircraft will be used. The NTSB suggests taking the flight review in the aircraft most frequently flown, or the most complicated aircraft for which you are rated.

- *The WINGS Program*

A person who has satisfactorily completed one or more phases of an FAA-sponsored pilot proficiency award program (the *WINGS* Program) meets the requirements of a flight review. This program was developed as a way to promote proficiency and safety, while providing a motivation for pilots to do so. What pilot doesn't feel satisfaction with an earned pair of wings?

It's a great program that gives pilots the opportunity to attend FAA safety seminars, participate in online courses—and be rewarded for meeting the regulatory requirements. See Appendix 4 and visit faasafety.gov for more information on the *WINGS* Program.

Conduct of the Flight Review

Although the regulation (14 CFR §61.56) does not specify which maneuvers should be included in a flight review, the FAA has provided some guidance to include suggested procedures. Ultimately the contents of a flight review are at the discretion of the flight instructor, but for a consistent and thorough check, consult AC 61-98D, and the FAA's Guidance Document: "Conducting an Effective Flight Review" (*see* Appendix 1).

The flight review should be conducted in an efficient manner, meeting the 1 hour ground and 1 hour flight requirement, without being excessive.

You may supplement this guide with other comprehensive study materials as noted in brackets at the end of each answer; for example [14 CFR 61.109]. The abbreviations and corresponding titles for these resources are listed below.

Be sure that you use the latest revision of these references when reviewing for the test. Also, check the ASA website at asa2fly.com/oegbfr for the most recent updates to this book due to

1 Introduction

changes in FAA procedures and regulations as well as for Reader Resources containing additional relevant information and updates.

14 CFR §21.97	*Approval of Major Changes in Type Design*
14 CFR Part 43	*Maintenance, preventive maintenance, rebuilding, and alteration*
14 CFR Part 61	*Certification: Pilots, flight instructors, and ground instructors*
14 CFR Part 68	*Requirements for Operating Certain Small Aircraft Without a Medical Certificate*
14 CFR Part 91	*General operating and flight rules*
14 CFR Part 107	*Operation and Certification of Small Unmanned Aircraft Systems*
NTSB Part 830	*49 CFR Part 830, Notification and Reporting of Aircraft Accidents and Incidents*
AC 61-91	*WINGS—Pilot Proficiency Program*
AC 61-98	*Currency Requirements and Guidance for the Flight Review*
AC 61-134	*General Aviation Controlled Flight Into Terrain Awareness*
AC 68-1	*BasicMed*
AC 90-109	*Transition to Unfamiliar Aircraft*
AC 91-73	*Parts 91 and 135 Single Pilot, Flight School Procedures During Taxi Operations*
AC 91-78	*Use of Class 1 or 2 Electronic Flight Bag (EFB)*
AC 107-2	*Small Unmanned Aircraft Systems (sUAS)*
AC 120-76	*Authorization for Use of Electronic Flight Bags*
AIM	*Aeronautical Information Manual*
ALC-25	*Flight Review Prep Guide*
AWC	*Aviation Weather Center (aviationweather.gov)*
FAA-H-8083-2	*Risk Management Handbook*
FAA-H-8083-3	*Airplane Flying Handbook*
FAA-H-8083-9	*Aviation Instructor's Handbook*
FAA-H-8083-15	*Instrument Flying Handbook*

(continued)

1 Introduction

FAA-H-8083-16	*Instrument Procedures Handbook*
FAA-H-8083-19	*Plane Sense: General Aviation Information*
FAA-H-8083-25	*Pilot's Handbook of Aeronautical Knowledge*
FAA-H-8083-28	*Aviation Weather Handbook*
Order 8900.1	*Flight Standards Information Management System (FSIMS)*
FAA NOTAM	*NOTAM Overview (faa.gov/about/office_org /headquarters_offices/ato/service_units /systemops/fs/alaskan/alaska/fai/notam /ntm_overview)*
FAA OTC	*Over-the-Counter (OTC) Medications Reference Guide (faa.gov/pilots/medical _certification/media/OTCMedicationsforPilots .pdf)*
FAA CBO	*Recreational Flyers & Modeler Community-Based Organizations (faa.gov/uas/recreational _fliers)*
FAA Safety	*Safety Briefing, March/April 2015, "Your Safety Reserve: Developing Your Personal Minimums" (faa.gov/sites/faa.gov/files/2022-01 /Personal-Minimums.pdf)*
TSA	*Transportation Security Administration (tsa.gov)*

Most of these documents are available on the FAA website (faa.gov). Additionally, many of the publications are printed by ASA (asa2fly.com) and are available from aviation retailers worldwide.

Q&A:
Questions Most Commonly Asked About the Flight Review

2

Chapter 2 Q&A: Questions About the Flight Review

Candidate Information

1. Who must take the flight review?

All pilots who wish to exercise their pilot-in-command (PIC) privilege and do not meet the exemptions listed below. A pilot would be in violation of 14 CFR §61.56 if they act as pilot-in-command after the expiration date of the flight review.

2. What procedures would exempt a pilot from the flight review requirement?

The following serve as exemptions from the flight review:
- 14 CFR §61.58 pilot proficiency check.
- 14 CFR Part 121 pilot proficiency check.
- 14 CFR Part 135 pilot proficiency check.
- 14 CFR Part 141 chief pilot proficiency check.
- Military pilot proficiency check.
- Any proficiency check administered by the FAA.
- Pilot examiner annual flight check.
- A passed practical test for any certificate or rating for which a new temporary airman certificate was issued.
- Procedures specifically authorized by the FAA.
- Satisfactory completion of any full phase of the FAA *WINGS* program.

[14 CFR 61.56]

3. Who can issue a flight review to an FAA certificated pilot?

Any current FAA certificated flight instructor or other person designated by the FAA.

4. Is the FAA notified of an unsuccessful flight review to an FAA certificated pilot?

No. The logbook endorsement states only satisfactory completion of the flight review. If the person issuing the flight review does not give the pilot the required endorsement, that pilot has the option of getting some dual instruction in the inadequate areas, or taking the flight review with another flight instructor.

Chapter 2   Q&A: Questions About the Flight Review

5. Can an instrument proficiency check (IPC) serve as a flight review?

While an IPC is a currency validation event, because it does not require ground training, it does not necessarily meet the requirements of the ground portion of a flight review. A flight review additionally requires more than an hour of flight in the air, and it is possible that an IPC may be completed in less time than the requisite hour for a flight review. So, an IPC does not automatically count for a flight review. A CFI and the student might choose to conduct an IPC that does include ground training and more than an hour of flight training that could additionally meet the requirements of a flight review concurrently. If this is done, the CFI would need to give each endorsement (a flight review and an IPC) separately.

6. Do student pilots require a flight review?

No. Flight reviews are required only by pilots holding a sport, recreational, private, commercial, flight instructor, or airline transport pilot certificate.

7. Why are flight reviews required?

The purpose of the flight review is to assess a pilot's skills in performing a *safe* flight.

8. A pilot's last flight review was completed on 08/01/2024. When will it expire?

Flight reviews are current for 24 calendar months to the end of the month. This flight review would expire 08/31/2026, or the last day of the month.

9. If a pilot has not had a flight review for more than two years, is his/her pilot certificate invalid?

No. Pilot certificates are issued for life, or until surrendered, suspended or revoked. Without a current flight review, however, the pilot may not act as PIC of an aircraft.

Chapter 2 Q&A: Questions About the Flight Review

10. Can a pilot fly solo (be the sole occupant of the airplane) without a current flight review?

No. Solo flight requires the pilot to act as PIC which is illegal without a current flight review.

11. Does a pilot have to possess a current medical certificate to satisfactorily complete a flight review?

No. But the pilot may not act as PIC, either during the flight review or any time thereafter, until medical eligibility has been obtained. This is a driver's license for sport pilot, BasicMed compliance (per 14 CFR Part 68), or a Third Class Medical Certificate (per 14 CFR Part 67). In such a case, the CFI conducting the flight review would be the PIC while the pilot demonstrated their abilities in accordance with the flight review being administered in "an aircraft for which that pilot is rated." This would not be the case if they are acting as a student pilot.

12. What do recreational/private pilots and higher need in order to fly light-sport aircraft (LSA)?

Your existing pilot's license is also your sport pilot certificate—no new certification is needed. If your medical has expired, you can use your driver's license as your medical eligibility to fly LSA. A pilot who has had a medical revoked or denied cannot use their driver's license to be eligible to fly an LSA aircraft. A pilot needs to have a medical certificate issued at First, Second, or Third Class to be eligible to be the PIC. Additionally, a pilot may not operate on BasicMed if they have had a medical revoked or denied.

[AC 68.1]

13. If a flight review is rendered unsatisfactory, does the pilot have to return to the same flight instructor for another attempt?

No. The pilot has the choice of using any authorized instructor.

Chapter 2 **Q&A: Questions About the Flight Review**

14. **Without a current flight review, may an instructor endorse a pilot's logbook for solo flight to prepare for the flight review?**

    No. Solo flight requires the pilot to act as PIC which is illegal without a current flight review. This would not be necessary anyway, because the flight review is not a test, but rather an instructional flight assessing the pilot's skills in performing a safe flight.

15. **If a pilot is presently taking dual lessons, do they have to take a flight review?**

    Yes. Dual lessons can only qualify as a flight review if the flight instructor conducts the lesson with those intentions, meets the requirements specified in 14 CFR §61.56, and issues the endorsement after a satisfactory completion of the flight.

16. **Can a pilot ask a flight instructor for a flight review endorsement without actually flying the review?**

    No. As required by 14 CFR §61.56, 1 hour of flight and 1 hour of ground training is required to qualify as a flight review.

    [14 CFR 61.56]

17. **Does a pilot have to get a flight review in each category and class of aircraft for which they are rated?**

    No. The satisfactory completion of the flight review allows pilots to exercise PIC privileges in all categories and classes of aircraft for which they are rated. Specifically, it is noted that a flight review must be "administered in an aircraft for which that pilot is rated." This does not indicate that a pilot would need to complete a flight review in each or all aircraft for which they are certificated. However, since safety is the main issue, pilots may elect to get a flight review in each category and class held on their pilot certificates. A good best practice for a pilot who is certificated for multiple categories and/or classes of aircraft might be to alternate the aircraft in which they complete a flight review or even get yearly flight review to guarantee proficiency.

Chapter 2 **Q&A: Questions About the Flight Review**

18. Does the flight review have to include all the maneuvers contained in the Airman Certification Standards (ACS) or Practical Test Standards (PTS)?

No. The pilot is required to perform only those maneuvers and procedures determined by the flight instructor as necessary to demonstrate the safe exercise of the privileges of the pilot certificate. However, this implies that the pilot should be able to perform at the level recognized by each certificate. *See* Pages 138 and 139.

19. Is there a written examination required by the FAA for completion of a flight review?

No. There is not a requirement for a written; however, the candidate must demonstrate knowledge of the general operating and flight rules of Part 91, and the flight instructor may choose to do this through a written or oral exercise. Many flight instructors ask candidates to complete a short written review before meeting to complete the flight review. *See* Page 133.

Another option is for the applicant to complete the FAA's online course for the flight review. This scenario-based multiple-choice quiz reviews Part 91 and the AIM in preparation for your next flight review. Upon successful completion of the course you can print a certificate of achievement. This course is available at faasafety.gov; select the Learning Center tab, and follow the links for the available Online Courses.

20. How can a pilot prove satisfactory completion of a flight review?

The satisfactory completion of a flight review requires the pilot receive an endorsement by the flight instructor giving the review. The pilot could choose to keep this in a training record, their logbook, or a digital logbook for their own record keeping.

The endorsement recommended in the FAA AC 61-56 would include the following:

I certify that (First name, MI, Last name), (pilot certificate), (certificate number), has satisfactorily completed a flight review of §61.56(a) on (date).

S/S   [date]   J.J. Jones   987654321 CFI   Exp. 01-31-2026

Chapter 2 Q&A: Questions About the Flight Review

21. Does the logbook endorsement mean the pilot must carry his/her logbook at all times as proof of the completion of the flight review?

No. The pilot must be able to present the endorsement only when asked by an authority, such as the FAA, NTSB, or a law enforcement officer, for the purpose of demonstrating eligibility for a practical test with an examiner. The endorsement may also be asked for by a flight instructor who is providing additional training to a pilot or by an agent of a flight training provider, aircraft club, or even an insurance company for the purposes of demonstrating eligibility to use an aircraft or compliance with an insurance policy.

Note: Sport pilots must carry with them a logbook endorsement (a copy or separate card is sometimes used so the pilot does not have to carry the complete logbook) of their category/class of aircraft, but not the flight review.

22. How should the flight review be logged?

If the pilot is the sole manipulator of the controls, then the flight should be logged as PIC time. If receiving dual instruction, then the CFI should additionally log the time with the pilot as dual received. The pilot-in-command should be determined between the candidate and the flight instructor before beginning the review flight.

23. Must the aircraft being used be IFR equipped?

An aircraft need not be IFR equipped for a flight review. Flight reviews do not require that the pilot demonstrate instrument proficiency. However, if the pilot or CFI intend to do any instrument maneuvers or procedures the aircraft must be equipped with the instruments required for the type of flight operations intended. This should be discussed between the flight instructor and candidate during the preflight phase of the review.

Chapter 2 **Q&A: Questions About the Flight Review**

24. Must the aircraft have dual controls?

Dual controls are not required to be present for a flight review. However, if the airplane does not have dual controls, the pilot must be qualified to act as PIC with medical eligibility and be current (within the 24 month flight review window). The aircraft is required to have rudder pedals at both stations.

[14 CFR 91.109]

25. Can a ground trainer be used exclusively for the flight review?

Yes. A flight simulator or flight training device may be used as long as it meets the following requirements: the ground trainer must be used in accordance with an approved course under 14 CFR Part 142; it must be approved for landings; and it must represent an aircraft for which the pilot is rated.

Instructor Information

26. Who acts as PIC during the flight review?

The pilot-in-command should be determined prior to the flight so there is a clear understanding of responsibilities. This decision should be made after inspecting the pilot's logbook, pilot certificate, and medical certificate to ensure the candidate is qualified to act as PIC. If the pilot's flight review currency has elapsed, the CFI must act as the PIC for the flight.

27. What is the minimum time required for a satisfactory flight review?

14 CFR §61.56 requires 1 hour of flight and 1 hour of ground training.

28. What subjects should be covered during the ground training?

The FAA specifies only a knowledge of 14 CFR Part 91. The objective of the flight review is safe flight by the candidate, so each ground training should be tailored to the pilot's experience, and type of flight normally conducted. This is a

Chapter 2 Q&A: Questions About the Flight Review

learning experience—the training should be broad enough to be comprehensive, yet have enough depth to provide a forum for learning.

Good resources for a pilot to refer to when preparing for a flight review are the FAA's online course that is eligible for FAA Wings credit (ALC-25: Flight Review Prep Guide), available at faasafety.gov and/or by reviewing AC 61-98 *Currency Requirements and Guidance for the Flight Review.*

[AC 61-98, ALC-25]

29. What maneuvers are required during the flight portion of the flight review?

The FAA specifies only those maneuvers and procedures which, at the discretion of the person giving the review, are necessary for the pilot to demonstrate the safe exercise of the privileges of the pilot certificate. AC 61-98 and the Flight Review Checklist provide more specific advice as to the conduct of the flight review.

30. Which ratings are required for a flight instructor to conduct flight reviews?

A flight instructor must be certificated with the pilot and flight instructor certificate in both the category and class of aircraft in which they will be operating to conduct a flight review.

31. Must the flight instructor possess a current medical certificate to conduct a flight review?

A flight instructor is not required to be the PIC of the aircraft during a flight review. If the CFI is not, the pilot receiving the flight review must be currently able to act as PIC of the aircraft. This would mean that the pilot receiving the flight review must have a current flight review in the category and class of aircraft to be used for the flight review at the time it is conducted. Who is eligible to be and will be PIC should be determined in the preflight phase if the pilot is qualified and able to satisfy this requirement.

32. Is the flight instructor required to have experience in each make and model of aircraft in which the flight review is going to be conducted?

No limitations on CFIs providing training required for a flight review are offered in 14 CFR §61.195 (Flight instructor limitations and qualifications), as long as the CFI is certificated in the category and/or class of aircraft regarding make and model experience requirements. A CFI may provide flight reviews in any aircraft of a category and/or class for which they are certificated, but they are advised that experience in make and model may be a wise safety consideration when conducting a flight review.

[14 CFR 61.195]

33. What responsibilities does the flight instructor have following a flight review?

Upon completion of a flight review, the flight instructor should debrief the pilot and inform them whether the review was satisfactory or unsatisfactory. Either way, the candidate should be provided with a comprehensive analysis of their performance, including any weak areas. If the flight review was satisfactory, the candidate's logbook must be endorsed accordingly. If the review is unsatisfactory, no logbook endorsement should be made, but the CFI should sign the pilot's logbook for any dual instruction given as they would any normal dual instructional flight.

34. How should the flight time be logged by the flight instructor?

The flight instructor should log the flight review as PIC time, as per 14 CFR §61.51(e)(3).

35. Is the instructor required to keep a record of all flight reviews administered?

No, it is not required; however, it is highly recommended that they do so.

[14 CRF 61.189]

36. Are flight instructors required to get flight reviews?

Yes. Unless they meet the exemptions listed in question 2, all pilots are required to meet the flight review requirement.

37. Can a flight instructor endorse their own logbook for the satisfactory completion of a flight review?

No. According to 14 CFR §61.195(i) and §61.421, flight instructors shall not make any self-endorsement for a certificate, rating, flight review, authorization, operating privilege, practical test, or knowledge test.

38. Do flight instructors have to go to the FAA for a flight review?

No. Any authorized flight instructor may conduct the flight review.

39. Do flight instructor refresher courses (FIRC) serve as a flight review?

No. Refresher courses do not meet all of the flight review requirements; however, they do meet the one hour ground training requirement.

Ground Instruction Requirement 3

Chapter 3   **Ground Instruction Requirement**

There is a 1 hour requirement for ground training dictated by 14 CFR §61.56 that involves the review of the current general operating and flight rules of 14 CFR Part 91. This can be accomplished in one of three ways: through an oral exercise, a written exercise, or a combination of both. The FAA's online Flight Review course (available at faasafety.gov) is an excellent way to meet the ground training requirement.

Review: Sample Oral Exercise
A. Privileges and Limitations
1. **To act as pilot-in-command or in any other capacity as a required flight crewmember of a civil aircraft, what documents must a pilot have in their physical possession or readily accessible in the aircraft?**
    a. A pilot certificate (or special purpose pilot authorization).
    b. An appropriate current medical certificate or alternate means of compliance with medical requirements (for example, balloon, glider, and LSA operations may be allowed while operating under BasicMed per 14 CFR Part 68 of with a valid state-issued driver's license as appropriate).
    c. A current and valid photo ID (such as a driver's license, government ID card, military ID card, or passport).
    [14 CFR 61.3]

2. **Can a pilot who is the holder of a recreational, private, commercial, or ATP pilot certificate, fly an aircraft without a current FAA medical certificate?**
    A pilot who has any of these certificates may not fly an aircraft without a Third, Second, or First Class Medical Certificate. Unless they are operating under the provision of BasicMed or unless it is an LSA aircraft, and they are exercising the privileges of sport pilot. A sport pilot certificate or exercising the privileges of sport pilot does not require a pilot to have an FAA issued medical certificate. They may operate under sport pilot restrictions In LSA qualified aircraft as long as they are the holder of a current state-issued driver's license.
    [14 CFR 61.23]

Chapter 3 Ground Instruction Requirement

3. If a pilot is the holder of a sport pilot certificate or exercising sport pilot, what privileges and limitations must they operate within in a light-sport aircraft?

Several limitations apply when a pilot is using a driver's license as medical eligibility and acting as a sport pilot. They include:

a. You can share the operating expenses of a flight with a passenger, provided the expenses involve only fuel, oil, airport expenses, or aircraft rental fees. You must pay at least half the operating expenses of the flight.

b. You *cannot* act as pilot-in-command of an LSA:
   - that is carrying a passenger or property for compensation or hire.
   - for compensation or hire.
   - in furtherance of a business.
   - while carrying more than one passenger.
   - at night.
   - in Class A airspace.
   - outside the U.S., unless you have prior authorization from the country in which you seek to operate. (Your sport pilot certificate carries the limit "Holder does not meet ICAO requirements.")
   - to demonstrate the aircraft in flight to a prospective buyer if you are an aircraft salesperson.
   - in a passenger-carrying airlift sponsored by a charitable organization.
   - at an altitude of more than 10,000 feet MSL.
   - when the flight or surface visibility is less than 3 statute miles.
   - without visual reference to the surface.
   - contrary to any operating limitation placed on the airworthiness certificate of the aircraft being flown.
   - contrary to any limit or endorsement on your pilot certificate, airman medical certificate, or any other limit or endorsement from an authorized instructor.
   - contrary to any restriction or limitation on your U.S. driver's license or any restriction or limitation imposed by judicial

(continued)

or administrative order when using your driver's license to satisfy a requirement of this part.
- while towing any object.
- as a pilot flight crewmember on any aircraft for which more than one pilot is required by the type certificate of the aircraft or the regulations under which the flight is conducted.

[14 CFR 61.315]

B. Medical Qualifications and Considerations

1. A pilot has received an FAA medical certificate from an airman medical examiner. How long is the medical valid before they will need a new medical?

A pilot receiving a First, Second, or Third Class Medical Certificate will have a valid medical certificate until the end of the expiration month, which depends on which class of medical certificate they received and their age.

The longest lasting is a Third Class Medical Certificate for pilots who are under the age of 40, which expires at the end of the 60th month after the month of the date of the examination shown on the medical certificate. For a pilot who is 40 or older, the same Third Class Medical Certificate expires at the end of the 24th month after the month of the date of the examination shown on the medical certificate.

A pilot who receives a First or Second Class Medical Certificate experiences shorter lengths of time that those medical certificates may be used for privileges that require First or Second Class Medical Certificate, but after those periods of time expire they may be used for lower level Third Class Medical Certificate privileges in accordance with normal validity durations of a Third Class Medical Certificate.

A First Class Medical Certificate is eligible to be used for those privileges for a pilot under the age of 40 until the 12th month after the month of the date of the examination shown on the medical certificate and until the 6th month after the month of the date of the examination shown on the medical certificate for a pilot 40 and older.

A Second Class Medical Certificate is eligible to be used for those privileges for a pilot under or over the age of 40 until the 12th month after the month of the date of the examination shown on the medical certificate.

[14 CFR 61.23]

2. What is BasicMed?

The FAA allows pilots to operate as PIC of certain covered aircraft without having to undergo the medical certification process under 14 CFR Part 67. The pilot and aircraft must meet certain prescribed conditions to operate under BasicMed, as defined in Part 68.

[14 CFR Part 68, AC 68-1]

3. What are the requirements to fly under BasicMed regulations?

A pilot must:

a. Hold a U.S. driver's license.

b. Hold or have held a medical certificate issued by the FAA at any point after July 15, 2006.

c. Answer the health questions on the Comprehensive Medical Examination Checklist (CMEC).

d. Undergo a physical examination by any state-licensed physician, and have that physician complete the CMEC. Keep the signed CMEC document.

e. Take an online medical education course and complete the attestations/consent to the National Driver Register (NDR) check. Keep the course completion documentation.

[14 CFR 61.23, AC 68-1]

Chapter 3 **Ground Instruction Requirement**

4. Explain the privileges and limitations of flying under BasicMed.

Pilots can conduct any operation that they would otherwise be able to conduct using their pilot certificate and a Third Class Medical Certificate, except they are limited to:

a. Fly with no more than five passengers.

b. Fly an aircraft under 6,000 lbs maximum certificated takeoff weight.

c. Fly an aircraft that is authorized to carry no more than six occupants.

d. Flights within the U.S., at an indicated airspeed of 250 knots or less, and at an altitude at or below 18,000 feet MSL.

e. May not fly for compensation or hire.

[14 CFR 61.113, AC 68-1]

5. What regulations apply and what common sense should prevail concerning the use of drugs and medication?

Pilot performance can be seriously degraded by both prescribed and over-the-counter medications, as well as by the medical conditions for which they are taken. The regulations prohibit pilots from performing crewmember duties while using any medication that affects the faculties in any way contrary to safety. The safest rule is not to fly as a crewmember while taking any medication, unless approved to do so by the FAA.

[14 CFR 91.17]

6. How may a pilot determine if an over-the-counter medication can be taken and still allow a pilot to fly? Or how long they should wait until they fly again?

The FAA has offered documents that help pilots determine if medication adversely affects their ability to fly. In the FAA's guide, key factors relate to if the medication has notices about operating machinery, may cause drowsiness, or has potential symptoms that can affect a pilot's ability to perform required tasks. Key considerations listed include:

Chapter 3 **Ground Instruction Requirement**

- In the last five days, have you taken, or do you plan to take any medications before flying?
- If currently taking a medication only for symptom relief, would you be safe to fly without it?
- Do you have any other underlying health conditions?

Generally, the FAA recommends a period of time at least 5 times the length of dosage period to elapse before a pilot would fly. In such an example, a medication that was taken every 8 hours (or three times daily) would require a pilot to wait at least 40 hours before flying.

[FAA OTC]

7. Spring has finally arrived and the weather looks great so you decide to rent an airplane and go fly. Your allergies are giving you issues and you have just taken medication to relieve your symptoms. Can you still fly?

The safe decision is to not fly while taking any medication, unless approved to do so by the FAA. Some of the most commonly used OTC drugs to treat seasonal allergies, antihistamines and decongestants, have the potential to cause noticeable adverse side effects, including drowsiness and cognitive deficits. 14 CFR §91.17 prohibits pilots from performing crewmember duties while using any medication that affects the body in any way contrary to safety. If there is any doubt regarding the effects of any medication, consult an Aviation Medical Examiner (AME) before flying.

[14 CFR 61.53, 91.17, FAA-H-8083-25]

8. Where can you find a list of the medical conditions that may disqualify you from obtaining a medical certificate?

The standards for medical certification are contained in 14 CFR Part 67 and the requirements for obtaining medical certificates can be found in Part 61.

[14 CFR Part 67, FAA-H-8083-25]

Chapter 3 Ground Instruction Requirement

9. **Explain the use of a personal checklist such as I'M SAFE to determine personal risks.**

    Personal, self-assessment checklists assist pilots in conducting preflight checks on themselves, reviewing their physical and emotional states that could have an effect on their performance. The I'M SAFE checklist reminds pilots to consider the following:

    Illness—Do I have any symptoms?

    Medication—Have I been taking prescription or over-the-counter drugs?

    Stress—Am I under psychological pressure from my job? Do I have money, family or health problems?

    Alcohol—Have I been drinking within 8 hours? Within 24 hours?

    Fatigue—Am I tired and not adequately rested?

    Eating—Am I adequately nourished?

    [FAA-H-8083-2]

10. **What restrictions apply to pilots concerning the use of drugs and alcohol?**

    No person may act or attempt to act as a crewmember of a civil aircraft:

    a. within 8 hours after the consumption of any alcoholic beverage;

    b. while under the influence of alcohol;

    c. while having .04 percent by weight or more alcohol in the blood;

    d. while using any drug that affects the person's faculties in any way contrary to safety.

    [14 CFR 91.17]

11. **Is it permissible for a pilot to allow a person who is obviously under the influence of intoxicating liquors or drugs to be carried aboard an aircraft?**

    No. Except in an emergency, no pilot of a civil aircraft may allow a person who appears to be intoxicated or who demonstrates by manner or physical indications that the individual is under the influence of drugs (except a medical patient under proper care) to be carried in that aircraft.

    [14 CFR 91.17]

12. What should a pilot know about reporting requirements relating to an alcohol-related motor vehicle action (MVA)?

14 CFR §61.15(e) requires all Part 61 certificate holders to send a written report to the FAA within 60 calendar days of any drug- and/or alcohol-related MVA. These reports are commonly referred to as notification letters.

14 CFR §61.15(c), defines a motor vehicle action as:

- A conviction after November 29, 1990, for the violation of any federal or state statute relating to the operation of a motor vehicle while intoxicated by alcohol or a drug, while impaired by alcohol or a drug, or while under the influence of alcohol or a drug.

  Examples of reportable convictions (not a comprehensive list):
  - Driving under the influence (DUI)
  - Driving while impaired (DWI)
  - Driving with an unlawful blood alcohol level
  - Operating while under the influence (OWUI)

- The cancellation, suspension, or revocation of a license to operate a motor vehicle after November 29, 1990, for a cause related to the operation of a motor vehicle while intoxicated by alcohol or a drug, while impaired by alcohol or a drug, or while under the influence of alcohol or a drug.

  Examples of reportable administrative actions (not a comprehensive list):
  - Revocation, suspension, or cancellation of driver license for chemical test failure or chemical test refusal
  - Administrative per se orders
  - 10-day civil revocations
  - Express consent revocation/suspension

- The denial after November 29, 1990, of an application for a license to operate a motor vehicle for a cause related to the operation of a motor vehicle while intoxicated by alcohol or a drug, while impaired by alcohol or a drug, or while under the influence of alcohol or a drug.

Chapter 3 **Ground Instruction Requirement**

C. Currency Requirements

1. What are the requirements to remain current as a private pilot?

   a. Accomplish a flight review given in an aircraft for which that pilot is rated by an authorized instructor within the preceding 24 calendar months.

   b. To carry passengers, a pilot must have made within the preceding 90 days:
   - Three takeoffs and three landings as the sole manipulator of the flight controls of an aircraft of the same category and class and, if a type rating is required, of the same type.
   - If the aircraft is a tailwheel airplane, the landings must have been made to a full stop.
   - If operations are to be conducted during the period beginning 1 hour after sunset to 1 hour before sunrise, with passengers on board, the pilot-in-command must have, within the preceding 90 days, made at least three takeoffs and three landings to a full stop during that period in an aircraft of the same category, class, and type (if a type rating is required) of aircraft to be used.

[14 CFR 61.56, 61.57]

2. Explain the difference between being current and being proficient.

Being current means that a pilot has accomplished the minimum FAA regulatory requirements within a specific time period to exercise the privileges of their certificate. It means that a pilot may legally fly, but does not necessarily mean that they're proficient or competent to conduct that flight.

Being proficient means that a pilot is capable of conducting a flight with a high degree of competence and that the pilot has a wide range of aeronautical knowledge and skills. Being proficient is not just about being current in terms of the regulations; it is about flying smart and safe. Be able to discuss how you will maintain proficiency, how you might adjust personal minimums, and how you will make go/no-go decisions based on your recency of flight experience.

Chapter 3 Ground Instruction Requirement

The FAA's WINGS: Pilot Proficiency Programs (AC 61-91) can offer pilots help with resources to maintain proficiency and plan to go beyond basic currency.

[FAA-H-8083-2, AC 61-91, FAA Safety]

3. How will establishing a personal minimums checklist reduce risk?

Professional pilots live by the numbers, and so should you. Pre-established hard numbers can make it a lot easier to make a smart go/no-go or divert decision than a vague sense that you can probably deal with the conditions that you are facing at any given time. In addition, a written set of personal minimums can also make it easier to explain tough decisions to passengers who are, after all, trusting their lives to your aeronautical skill and judgment.

[FAA-H-8083-25, FAA Safety]

4. The airplane you normally rent has been grounded due to an intermittent electrical problem. You ask to be scheduled in another airplane. During preflight of the new airplane, you discover that it has avionics you're unfamiliar with. Should you go ahead and depart on your VFR flight?

Pilot familiarity with all equipment is critical in optimizing both safety and efficiency. A pilot's unfamiliarity with any aircraft system will add to their workload and may contribute to a loss of situational awareness. Pilots should regard unfamiliarity with the aircraft and its systems as a hazard with high risk potential. This level of proficiency is critical and should be looked upon as a requirement, not unlike carrying an adequate supply of fuel. Discipline is the key to success. The FAA offers an advisory circular (AC 90-109A) that can help pilots identify strategies, risks, and methodologies for transitioning to unfamiliar aircraft.

[FAA-H-8083-2, AC 90-109A]

Chapter 3 **Ground Instruction Requirement**

D. Aircraft Certificates and Documents

1. What documents are required on board an aircraft prior to flight?

Supplements (14 CFR §91.9)
Placards (14 CFR §91.9)
Airworthiness Certificate (14 CFR §91.203)
Registration Certificate (14 CFR §91.203)
Radio Station License—if operating outside of U.S.; FCC regulation (47 CFR §87.18)
Operating limitations—AFM/POH and supplements, placards, markings (14 CFR §91.9)
Weight and balance data—current (14 CFR §23.2620)
Compass Deviation Card (14 CFR §23.1547)
External Data Plate/Serial Number (14 CFR §45.11)

Exam Tip: During the practical test, your evaluator may wish to examine the various required aircraft documents (SPARROW) during the preflight inspection, as well as the currency of any aeronautical charts, EFB data, etc., on board the aircraft. Prior to the test, verify that all of the necessary aircraft documentation, onboard databases, charts, etc., are current and available.

[14 CFR 91.203, 91.9]

2. Does an airworthiness certificate have an expiration date?

No. A standard airworthiness certificate remains valid for as long as the aircraft meets its approved type design, is in a condition for safe operation, and the maintenance, preventive maintenance, and alterations are performed in accordance with Parts 21, 43, and 91.

[FAA-H-8083-25]

3. What is an airworthiness certificate?

An airworthiness certificate is issued by the FAA to all aircraft that have been proven to meet the minimum requirements of Part 21 and that are in condition for safe operation. Under any circumstances, the aircraft must meet the requirements of the original Type Certificate, or it is no longer airworthy.

Chapter 3 Ground Instruction Requirement

Airworthiness certificates come in two different classifications: standard airworthiness and special airworthiness.

[FAA-H-8083-25]

4. What is an aircraft registration certificate?

Before an aircraft can be flown legally, it must be registered with the FAA Aircraft Registry. The Certificate of Aircraft Registration, which is issued to the owner as evidence of the registration, must be carried in the aircraft at all times.

[FAA-H-8083-25]

5. Does an aircraft's registration certificate have an expiration date?

Yes. A Certificate of Aircraft Registration issued in accordance with 14 CFR §47.31 expires seven years after the last day of the month in which it was issued. A temporary Certification of Registration is valid for up to 12 months after the date the applicant signs the application.

Note: Effective January 23, 2023, if your registration certificate expires after this date, the registration certificate will automatically be extended an additional 4 years to allow for a total of 7 years. Prior to January 23, 2023, registration certificates were valid for 3 years.

[14 CFR 47.40]

6. Where must the airworthiness certificate be located?

The certificate must be displayed at the cabin or cockpit entrance so that it is legible to passengers or crew.

[14 CFR 91.203, FAA-H-8083-19]

7. For an aircraft to be considered airworthy, what two conditions must be met?

  a. The aircraft must conform to its type design (type certificate). Conformity to type design is attained when the required components are installed consistent with the drawings, specifications, and other data that are part of the type certificate. Conformity includes applicable Supplemental Type Certificate(s) (STC) and field-approval alterations.

b. The aircraft must not show signs of wear and deterioration and be determined in condition for safe operation.

[FAA-H-8083-19]

E. Aircraft Maintenance Requirements

1. Who is responsible for determining whether an aircraft is airworthy and that all documents are present for a particular flight?

The PIC of a civil aircraft is responsible for determining whether that aircraft is in a condition for safe flight. The PIC shall discontinue the flight when unairworthy, mechanical, electrical, or structural conditions occur.

[14 CFR 91.403, 91.7]

2. Who is responsible for ensuring that an aircraft is maintained in an airworthy condition?

The owner or operator of an aircraft is primarily responsible for maintaining an aircraft in an airworthy condition.

[14 CFR 91.403]

3. What records or documents should be checked to determine that the owner or operator of an aircraft has complied with all required inspections and airworthiness directives?

The maintenance records (aircraft and engine logbooks). Each owner or operator of an aircraft shall ensure that maintenance personnel make appropriate entries in the aircraft maintenance records indicating the aircraft has been approved for return to service.

[14 CFR 91.405]

4. Explain how a pilot determines that an aircraft conforms to its approved type design and is in a condition for safe operation.

To determine that the aircraft conforms to its type design a pilot must determine that the maintenance, preventive maintenance, and alterations have been performed in accordance 14 CFR Parts 21, 43, and 91, and that the aircraft is registered in the United States. The pilot does this by ensuring that all required inspections, maintenance, preventive maintenance, repairs, and alterations have been appropriately documented in the aircraft's maintenance records.

To determine that the aircraft is in condition for safe operation the pilot conducts a thorough preflight inspection by inspecting the aircraft for wear and deterioration, structural damage, fluid leaks, tire wear, inoperative instruments and equipment, etc. If an unsafe condition exists or inoperative instruments or equipment are found, the pilot must use the guidance in 14 CFR §91.213 to handle the inoperative equipment.

5. What regulations apply concerning the operation of an aircraft that has had alterations or repairs which may have substantially affected its operation in flight?

No person may operate or carry passengers in any aircraft that has undergone maintenance, preventive maintenance, rebuilding, or alteration that may have appreciably changed its flight characteristics or substantially affected its operation in flight until an appropriately rated pilot with at least a private pilot certificate:

a. Flies the aircraft;

b. Makes an operational check of the maintenance performed or alteration made; and

c. Logs the flight in the aircraft records.

[14 CFR 91.407]

Chapter 3 **Ground Instruction Requirement**

6. **During the preflight inspection in an aircraft that doesn't have a MEL (minimum equipment list) or KOEL (kinds of operation list), you notice that an instrument or equipment item is inoperative. Describe how you will determine if the aircraft is still airworthy for flight.**

    I will ask myself the following questions to determine if I can legally fly the airplane with the inoperative equipment item:

    a. Are the inoperative instruments or equipment part of the VFR-day type certification?

    b. Are the inoperative instruments or equipment listed as required on the aircraft's equipment list or kinds of operations equipment list (KOEL) for the kind of flight operation being conducted?

    c. Are the inoperative instruments or equipment required by 14 CFR §91.205, §91.207, or any other rule of Part 91 for the specific kind of flight operation being conducted (e.g., VFR, IFR, day, night)?

    d. Are the inoperative instruments or equipment required to be operational by an AD?

    If the answer is yes to any of these questions, the aircraft is not airworthy, and maintenance is required before I can fly. If the answer is no to all these questions, then the inoperative instruments or equipment must be removed (by an A&P) from the aircraft or be deactivated and placarded inoperative.

    [14 CFR 91.213(d), FAA-H-8083-25]

7. **Can you legally fly an aircraft that has an inoperative flap position indicator?**

    Unless operations are conducted under 14 CFR §91.213, the regulations require that all equipment installed on an aircraft in compliance with either the Airworthiness Standards or the Operating Rules must be operative. If equipment originally installed in the aircraft is no longer operative, the Airworthiness Certificate is not valid until such equipment is either repaired or removed from that aircraft. *See next question for an exception.*

    However, the rules also permit the publication of a minimum equipment list (MEL) where compliance with these equipment requirements is not necessary in the interest of safety under all conditions. Deviation from the equipment requirements of the regulation is maintained by alternate means. Experience has shown that with the various levels of redundancy designed into aircraft, operation of every system or component installed may not be necessary when the remaining operative equipment can provide an acceptable level of safety.

8. **What responsibilities should a pilot be familiar with concerning inoperative equipment on the aircraft?**

   a. No person may take off in an aircraft with inoperative instruments or equipment installed unless:
      - An approved minimum equipment list exists for that aircraft;
      - A letter of authorization from the FAA is carried within the aircraft authorizing use of a MEL; and
      - The aircraft records available to the pilot must include an entry describing the inoperable instruments and equipment allowed by the MEL.

   Or:

   b. A person may take off in an aircraft with inoperative instruments and equipment without an approved minimum equipment list provided:
      - The flight operation is conducted in a non-turbine powered aircraft for which a Master minimum equipment list has not been developed; and
      - The inoperable instruments and equipment are not part of the VFR-day type certification instruments and equipment prescribed in the applicable airworthiness regulations; and
      - The inoperable instruments and equipment are removed from the aircraft or made inoperative, the cockpit control placarded, the change is recorded by an authorized maintenance provider; and
      - A determination is made by a certificated, appropriately rated pilot and/or mechanic that the inoperative instruments or equipment do not constitute a hazard to the aircraft.

[14 CFR 91.213]

9. What are the required maintenance inspections for aircraft?

No person may operate an aircraft unless, within the preceding 12 calendar months, it has had an annual inspection in accordance with 14 CFR Part 43 and has been approved for return to service. Also, no person may operate an aircraft carrying any person (other than a crewmember) for hire, and no person may give flight instruction for hire in an aircraft which that person provides, unless within the preceding 100 hours of time in service the aircraft has received an annual or 100-hour inspection and has been approved for return to service.

Note: Be capable of locating the 100-hour and annual inspections in the aircraft and engine logbooks.

[14 CFR 91.409]

10. How often must the transponder in an aircraft be tested and inspected?

No person may use an ATC transponder unless it has been tested and inspected within the preceding 24 calendar months.

[14 CFR 91.413]

11. What responsibilities does an owner or operator have concerning maintenance records for their aircraft?

Each registered owner or operator shall keep records of the maintenance, preventive maintenance, and alteration and records of the 100-hour, annual, progressive, and other required or approved inspections, as appropriate, for each aircraft (including the airframe) and each engine propeller, rotor and appliance of an aircraft. The records must include:

a. A description (or reference to data acceptable to the Administrator) of the work performed;

b. The date of completion of the work performed;

c. The signature and certificate number of the person approving the aircraft for return to service; and also

d. A record of the preventive maintenance must be entered in the maintenance records.

[14 CFR 91.417]

Chapter 3 Ground Instruction Requirement

12. **Define *preventive maintenance*.**

    Preventive maintenance items which can be performed by the pilot are listed in 14 CFR Part 43 and include such basic items as oil changes, wheel bearing lubrication, and hydraulic fluid (brakes, landing gear system) refills. However, even if Part 43 permits certain work, do not exceed your personal skill level. 14 CFR Part 43, Appendix A(c) includes a list of preventive maintenance work that a pilot may be able to conduct as long as it does not involve complex assembly operations.

    [14 CFR Part 43]

13. **What are special flight permits, and when are they necessary?**

    A special flight permit may be issued for an aircraft that may not currently meet applicable airworthiness requirements but is capable of safe flight. These permits are typically issued for the following purposes:

    a. Flying an aircraft to a base where repairs, alterations or maintenance are to be performed, or to a point of storage.
    b. Delivering or exporting an aircraft.
    c. Production flight testing new-production aircraft.
    d. Evacuating aircraft from areas of impending danger.
    e. Conducting customer demonstration flights in new-production aircraft that have satisfactorily completed production flight tests.

    [14 CFR 21.197, 91.213]

14. **How are special flight permits obtained?**

    If a special flight permit is needed, assistance and the necessary forms may be obtained from the local FSDO or Designated Airworthiness Representative (DAR). Applications for an airworthiness certificate can be submitted online via the Airworthiness Certification (AWC) tool.

    [FAA-H-8083-25]

Chapter 3 **Ground Instruction Requirement**

15. What are Airworthiness Directives (ADs)?

An AD is the medium the FAA uses to notify aircraft owners and other potentially interested persons of unsafe conditions that may exist because of design defects, maintenance, or other causes, and to specify the conditions under which the product may continue to be operated. ADs are regulatory in nature, and compliance is mandatory. It is the aircraft owner's or operator's responsibility to ensure compliance with all pertinent ADs. ADs are divided into two categories: Those of an emergency nature requiring immediate compliance prior to further flight and those of a less urgent nature requiring compliance within a specified period of time. All ADs and the AD Biweekly are free on the internet at drs.faa.gov/reports/ad-biweekly.

[FAA-H-8083-25]

16. Are electronic flight bags (EFBs) approved for use as a replacement for paper reference material (POH and supplements, etc.) in the cockpit?

Yes; EFBs can be used during all phases of flight operations in lieu of paper reference material when the information displayed is the functional equivalent of the paper reference material replaced and is current, up-to-date, and valid. It is recommended that a secondary or back-up source of aeronautical information necessary for the flight be available.

[AC 91-78, AC 120-76]

F. Weather

1. What are the different effects of stable and unstable air on clouds, turbulence, precipitation and visibility.

	Stable	Unstable
Clouds	Stratiform	Cumuliform
Turbulence	Smooth	Rough
Precipitation	Steady	Showery
Visibility	Fair to Poor	Good

[FAA-H-8083-28]

Chapter 3 **Ground Instruction Requirement**

2. **During preflight planning, what type of meteorological information should you be aware of with respect to icing?**
   a. *Location of fronts*—the front's location, type, speed, and direction of movement.
   b. *Cloud layers*—the location of cloud bases and tops; this is valuable when determining if you will be able to climb above icing layers or descend beneath those layers into warmer air.
   c. *Freezing level(s)*—important when determining how to avoid icing and how to exit icing conditions if accidentally encountered.
   d. *Air temperature and pressure*—icing tends to be found in low-pressure areas and at temperatures at or around freezing.
   e. *Precipitation*—knowing the location and type of precipitation forecast will assist in avoiding areas conducive to severe icing.

   Exam Tip: Know what your plan will be if you accidentally encounter in-flight icing. Be able to explain how you will determine the potential for icing during preflight planning. What weather products will you use on the ground and inflight to determine potential areas of icing? (GFA, CIP, FIP, prog charts, winds aloft, etc.)

   [AC 91-74]

3. **What is the definition of the term *freezing level* and how can you determine where that level is?**

   The freezing level is the lowest altitude in the atmosphere over a given location at which the air temperature reaches 0°C. It is possible to have multiple freezing layers when a temperature inversion occurs above the defined freezing level. Potential sources of icing information for determining its location are: GFA, PIREPS, AIRMETs, SIGMETs, convective SIGMETs, low-level significant weather charts, surface analysis (for frontal location and freezing precipitation) and winds and temperatures aloft (for air temperature at altitude). Pilots can use graphical data including freezing level graphics, the current icing product (CIP), and forecast icing product (FIP). These products are available at the NWS Aviation Weather Center website: aviationweather.gov/gfa/#ice.

   [FAA-H-8083-28]

Chapter 3 **Ground Instruction Requirement**

4. What is necessary for structural icing to occur?

The aircraft must be flying through visible water such as rain or cloud droplets; temperature must be at the point where moisture strikes the aircraft at 0°C or colder.

[FAA-H-8083-28]

5. What action is recommended if you inadvertently encounter icing conditions?

Aircraft icing remains a key aviation safety issue. Accident data has shown that pilots are (advertently and inadvertently) flying aircraft not certificated for flight in icing conditions into such conditions, often with fatal results. Even more disturbing are the numbers of accidents involving aircraft that are certificated for flight in icing conditions. Such accidents are often the result of pilot complacency, poor technique, poor understanding of the airplane's limitations, and performance in icing conditions, misconceptions of airplane and system icing certification, and a misunderstanding of icing terminology.

It is critically important for pilots to obtain the freezing levels for the areas in which they will be flying to be able to make educated decisions on how to exit icing conditions if they are encountered. It is also important for pilots to know if there are any temperature inversions aloft that might alter the normal relationship between altitude and air temperature. Pilots should be aware of multiple freezing levels and their locations.

Pilots in such aircraft should emphasize ice avoidance during preflight planning and pay special attention to planning an alternate course of action in case actual icing is encountered.

In the event of an inadvertent icing encounter, the pilot should take appropriate action to exit the conditions immediately, coordinating with air traffic control (ATC) as necessary, and declaring an emergency.

If an aircraft that is not approved for flight in icing conditions inadvertently encounters ice, controllers will not know if the aircraft is certificated or equipped for icing, the severity of the conditions, or what anti-icing or deicing equipment is installed on the aircraft.

[FAA-H-8083-28, AC 91-74A]

6. Is frost considered a hazard to flight? Why?

Yes, because even a small amount of frost on airfoils may prevent an aircraft from becoming airborne at normal takeoff speed.
It is also possible that, once airborne, an aircraft could have insufficient margin of airspeed above stall so that moderate gusts or turning flight could produce incipient or complete stalling.
Frost does not change the basic aerodynamics shape of the wing, but the roughness of its surface spoils the smooth flow of air, thus causing a slowing of airflow. This slowing of the air causes early airflow separation, resulting in a loss of lift. Further, "No pilot may take off an airplane that has frost, ice, or snow adhering to any propeller, windshield, or stabilizing or control surface; to a powerplant installation; or to an airspeed, altimeter, rate of climb, or flight attitude instrument system or wing, except that takeoffs may be made with frost under the wing in the area of the fuel tanks if authorized by the FAA."

[FAA-H-8083-28, 14 CFR 91.527]

7. What factors must be present for a thunderstorm to form?

a. A source of lift (heating, fast-moving front).
b. Unstable air (nonstandard lapse rate).
c. High moisture content (temperature/dew point close).

[FAA-H-8083-28]

8. Why is fog a major operational concern to pilots?

It is of primary concern during takeoffs and landings. Fog can reduce vertical and horizontal visibilities to zero-zero. It can occur instantly from a clear condition, making takeoffs, landings, and even taxiing, potentially hazardous operations.

[FAA-H-8083-28]

Chapter 3 Ground Instruction Requirement

9. What is wind shear and why is it an operational concern to pilots?

Wind shear is a change in wind speed and/or direction over a short distance. It can occur either horizontally or vertically and is most often associated with strong temperature inversions or density gradients. Wind shear can occur at high or low altitude. *Note:* This document discusses only low-altitude wind shear.

Four common sources of low-level wind shear are
1. Frontal activity.
2. Thunderstorms.
3. Temperature inversions.
4. Surface obstructions.

In its many forms, wind shear can change a routine approach into an emergency recovery in a matter of seconds.

An aircraft is affected by the change in wind direction/velocity because the wind also changes the aircraft motion relative to the ground. In some instances when low and when experiencing more violent shear, a recovery may not be possible in to avert damage.

Pilots are encouraged to manage wind shear hazards by:
- Knowing when wind shear is present or possible;
- Knowing the severity or magnitude of the change present or possible; and
- Being prepared to correct or go around immediately if wind shear is experienced.

[FAA-H-8083-28, FAA-P-8740-40]

10. What types of weather information will you examine to determine if wind shear conditions might affect your flight?

a. *Terminal forecasts*—any mention of low level wind shear (LLWS) or the possibility of severe thunderstorms, heavy rain showers, hail, and wind gusts suggest the potential for LLWS and microbursts.

b. *METARs*—inspect for any indication of thunderstorms, rain showers, or blowing dust. Additional signs such as warming trends, gusty winds, cumulonimbus clouds, etc., should be noted.

c. *Severe weather watch reports, SIGMETS, and convective SIGMETS*—severe convective weather is a prime source for wind shear and microbursts.

d. *LLWAS (low level wind shear alert system) reports*—installed at 110 airports in the U.S.; designed to detect wind shifts between outlying stations and a reference centerfield station.

e. *PIREPs*—reports of sudden airspeed changes on departure or approach and landing corridors provide a real-time indication of the presence of wind shear.

[FAA-H-8083-28]

11. **What is most likely to happen if a non-instrument rated pilot continues into IMC?**

    Inadvertent flight into IMC can lead to spatial disorientation and loss of control (LOC).

    [FAA-H-8083-15]

G. Obtaining Weather Information

1. **What process does the FAA recommend for obtaining a good weather briefing prior to a flight?**

    a. First get a big picture of weather patterns by watching television (The Weather Channel, etc.) and/or the internet several days prior to a flight.

    b. On the day or evening before a flight, obtain an outlook briefing from Flight Service and/or download weather and forecast charts from the internet.

    c. As close to departure time as possible, with preliminary flight planning complete (basic route, altitudes, preliminary alternates), call Flight Service or log on to 1800wxbrief for a standard briefing. A pilot can also access weather products on the internet or other sources (making sure the products are suitable for aviation use and are current).

    d. If a standard briefing is several hours prior to a flight or the weather is questionable, call an FSS for an abbreviated briefing just before takeoff.

    [FAA-P-8740-30]

Chapter 3 **Ground Instruction Requirement**

2. **What are some examples of other sources of weather information?**
   a. The Aviation Weather Center at aviationweather.gov
   b. Leidos Flight Services via the Internet. Pilots can receive preflight weather data and file domestic VFR and IFR flight plans: 1800wxbrief.com or call 1-800-WXBRIEF.
   c. Weather and aeronautical information available from numerous private industry sources.
   d. Flight Information Services (FIS-B via ADS-B In).

   [AIM 7-1-2, 7-1-8, 7-1-9, 7-1-11]

3. **What pertinent information should a weather briefing include?**
   a. Adverse conditions
   b. VFR flight not recommended
   c. Synopsis
   d. Current conditions
   e. Enroute forecast
   f. Destination forecast
   g. Winds aloft
   h. Notices to Air Missions (NOTAMs)
   i. ATC delay

   In addition, pilots may obtain the following from FSS briefers upon request: information on special use airspace (SUA) and SUA-related airspace, including alert areas, MOAs, MTRs (IFR, VFR, VR, and SR training routes), warning areas, and ATC assigned airspace (ATCAA); a review of the printed NOTAM publication; approximate density altitude data; information on air traffic services and rules; customs/immigration procedures; ADIZ rules; search and rescue; GPS RAIM availability for 1 hour before to 1 hour after ETA or a time specified by the pilot; and other assistance as required.

   [AIM 7-1-5]

Chapter 3 **Ground Instruction Requirement**

4. While en route, how can a pilot obtain updated weather information?

a. FSS on 122.2 or appropriate frequency; use of RCO frequency, if available.

b. ATIS/ASOS/AWOS.

c. Datalink weather—cockpit display of FIS-B information.

d. ATC (workload permitting).

Exam Tip: Be prepared to demonstrate how you would obtain in-flight weather advisories and updates and how you would communicate with an FSS while en route.

[FAA-H-8083-25]

5. What is Flight Information Service (FIS) and how does it work?

Flight Information Service–Broadcast (FIS-B) is a ground broadcast service provided through the Automatic Dependent Surveillance–Broadcast (ADS-B) services network over the 978 MHz Universal Access Transceiver (UAT) data link. The FAA FIS-B system provides pilots and flight crews of properly equipped aircraft with a flight deck display of aviation weather and aeronautical information.

[FAA-H-8083-25, AIM 7-1-11]

6. What are NOTAMs?

Notices to Air Missions (NOTAM)—Time critical aeronautical information, which is of either a temporary nature or not known sufficiently in advance to permit publication on aeronautical charts or in other operational publications, receives immediate dissemination via the Federal NOTAM System. It is aeronautical information that could affect a pilot's decision to make a flight. It includes such information as airport or primary runway closures, changes in the status of navigational aids, ILS's, radar service availability, and other information essential to planned en route, terminal, or landing operations.

[AIM 5-1-3]

Chapter 3 **Ground Instruction Requirement**

7. What are the different types of NOTAMs a pilot may encounter?

A Notice to Air Missions or NOTAM is a notice containing information (not known sufficiently in advance to publicize by other means) concerning the establishment, condition, or change in any component (facility, service, or procedure of, or hazard in the National Airspace System) that the timely knowledge of which is essential to personnel concerned with flight operations.

Several types of NOTAMS are used in the industry.

a. *Class I NOTAMs (ICAO)*—NOTAMs distributed by means of telecommunication.

b. *Class II NOTAMs (ICAO) or Published NOTAMs*—NOTAMs distributed by means other than telecommunications. In the United States these NOTAMs are published in the Notices to Air Missions Publication (NTAP) which is issued every 28 days.

c. *International NOTAMs*—Any NOTAM intended for distribution to more than one country would be considered an international NOTAM. However, an FSS does not have access to all international NOTAMs. For our purposes I will limit the definition to international NOTAMs that we at an FSS have access to. This would include NOTAMs stored in ICAO format in the United States NOTAM System (USNS) or published in the International NOTAMs section of the NTAP. The USNS stores international NOTAMs separately from domestic NOTAMs, but only for selected locations both inside and outside the United States. These NOTAMs are not included in a standard weather briefing unless specifically requested.

d. *Domestic NOTAMs*—NOTAMs that are primarily distributed within the United States although they may also be available in Canada. Domestic NOTAMs stored in the USNS are coded in a domestic format rather than an ICAO format.

e. *Civil NOTAMs*—Any NOTAM that is part of the civil NOTAM system which includes any NOTAM this is not part of the military NOTAM system.

f. *Military NOTAMs*—Any NOTAM that is part of the military NOTAM system which primarily includes NOTAMs on military airports and military airspace.

Chapter 3 **Ground Instruction Requirement**

g. *FDC NOTAMs*—Flight Data Center NOTAMs are NOTAMs that are regulatory in nature such as changes to an instrument approach procedure or airway. Temporary Flight Restrictions (TFRs) are also issued as FDC NOTAMs.

h. *Center Area NOTAMs*—An FDC NOTAM issued for a condition that is not limited to one airport, therefore it is filed under the Air Route Traffic Control Center (ARTCC) that controls the airspace involved. TFRs, airway changes and laser light activity are examples of this type of NOTAM. This becomes very important to know when looking for NOTAMs on your own. For example, you must retrieve ZAN FDC NOTAMs for flights in Alaska because ZAN is the code for Anchorage ARTCC which is the controlling Center for all of Alaska.

i. *NOTAM (D)*—A NOTAM given (in addition to local dissemination) distant dissemination beyond the area of responsibility of the Flight Service Station. This type of NOTAM now includes (U) NOTAMs and (O) NOTAMs. (U) NOTAMs are unverified NOTAMs which are those that are received from a source other than airport management and have not yet been confirmed by management personnel. This is allowed only at those airports where airport management has authorized it by Letter of Agreement. (O) NOTAMs are other aeronautical information which does not meet NOTAM criteria but may be beneficial to aircraft operations.

[FAA NOTAM, AIM 5-1-3]

8. Where can NOTAM information be obtained?

a. Call the flight service station 1800WXBRIEF.

b. NOTAM search: notams.aim.faa.gov/notamSearch/

c. Flight service flight briefing website: 1800wxbrief.com

d. Flight Information Services (FIS-B via ADS-B In).

Note: The NOTAM-D and NOTAM-FDC products broadcast via FIS-B are limited to those issued or effective within the past 30 days. Except for TFRs, NOTAMs older than 30 days are not provided.

[AIM 5-1-1, 5-1-3]

H. sUAS Operations and the General Aviation Pilot

1. What is a UAS NOTAM?

NOTAMs for uncrewed aircraft systems (UAS) are becoming more common and are of more importance to pilots in the National Airspace System than they have been historically. They might also potentially be referred to as DROTAMs. These cover areas that might include operations of unmanned aerial systems that are operating in the same airspace as other aircraft and are not necessarily prohibited or restricted airspaces.

Aviation authorities issue these NOTAMs to inform pilots of uncrewed aircraft systems or drones operating in a specific airspace area. The purpose of a UAS NOTAM is to provide a heads-up to manned aircraft pilots about the presence of drone operations within the designated airspace, promoting situational awareness and safety.

UAS NOTAMs typically include the following information:

a. *Location*—The geographic coordinates or reference points defining the area where drone operations are taking place.

b. *Altitude*—The vertical limits of the drone operation area, indicating the maximum and minimum altitudes where the UAS will be operating.

c. *Time of operation*—The date and time when the drone operation is scheduled to occur or when the airspace will be reserved for UAS activities.

d. *Type of operation*—Information about the nature of the drone operations, such as aerial photography, surveying, or other specific activities.

e. *Contact information*—The contact details of the entity or organization responsible for the drone operation, in case pilots need to obtain additional information or coordinate their flights.

UAS NOTAMs are typically published by air traffic control centers, flight service stations, or other relevant aviation authorities.

Chapter 3 Ground Instruction Requirement

2. What is a small uncrewed aircraft?

Small uncrewed aircraft (sUAS or drones) weigh less than 55 pounds (25 kg), including everything that is onboard or otherwise attached to the aircraft, and are operated without the possibility of direct human intervention from within or on the aircraft.

[14 CFR Part 107]

3. Who may operate an sUAS aircraft?

No person may manipulate the flight controls of a small uncrewed aircraft system unless:

(1) That person has a remote pilot certificate with a small UAS rating issued pursuant to subpart C of 14 CFR Part 107 and satisfies the requirements of §107.65; or

(2) That person is under the direct supervision of a remote pilot in command and the remote pilot in command has the ability to immediately take direct control of the flight of the sUAS.

[14 CFR 107.12, AC 107-2]

4. You are a crewed aircraft (airplane) pilot concerned about sUAS (drone) operations being conducted near your airport. Are drone operators required to obtain certification and/or permission from the FAA before flying their sUAS or drone in the National Airspace System?

There are two methods for sUAS (drone) fliers to operate within the National Airspace System in compliance with local laws, ordinances, and FAA regulations:

a. Fly in accordance with the rules established for recreational flyers and modeler community-based organizations.

b. Fly under the FAA's sUAS rules (Part 107).

[AC 107-2, FAA CBO]

Chapter 3 **Ground Instruction Requirement**

5. If a drone operator decides to fly under the FAA's sUAS rules (Part 107), what registration and certification rules must they adhere to?

Under 14 CFR Part 107, operators must:
- Register their drone with the FAA.
- Label their drone with their registration number.
- Obtain an FAA Remote Pilot Certificate.
- Follow the operational requirements of Part 107.

[14 CFR Part 107, AC 107-2]

6. What are the application requirements for both certificated pilots and non-certificated pilots to obtain a remote pilot certificate with a sUAS rating?

Applicants without a Part 61 pilot certificate must:
- Be at least 16 years of age.
- Be able to read, speak, write, and understand the English language.
- Be in a physical and mental condition that would not interfere with the safe operation of a sUAS.
- Pass an initial aeronautical knowledge test.
- Complete the remote pilot certificate and/or Rating Application FAA Form 8710-13 (online or paper).
- Pass a TSA vetting process.

Applicants with Part 61 pilot certificates must:
- Hold a pilot certificate issued under Part 61 (except a student pilot certificate).
- Have completed a flight review within the previous last 24 calendar months.
- Complete the Part 107 sUAS online training course (faasafety.gov).
- Complete the remote pilot certificate and/or Rating Application FAA Form 8710-13 (online or paper).
- Submit the training course graduation certificate to a Flight Standards Office, a DPE, an airman certification representative, or a CFI for identify verification.

[14 CFR Part 107, AC 107-2]

Chapter 3 **Ground Instruction Requirement**

7. Who has right of way in airspace, a sUAS operation or traditional aircraft?

(a) Each sUAS must yield the right of way to all aircraft, airborne vehicles, and launch and reentry vehicles. Yielding the right of way means that the sUAS must give way to the aircraft or vehicle and may not pass over, under, or ahead of it unless well clear.

(b) No person may operate an sUAS so close to another aircraft as to create a collision hazard.

[14 CFR 107.37]

8. When a pilot is operating in airspace, what should they know about where sUAS aircraft may be operating?

sUAS may operate in controlled or uncontrolled airspace. Operations in Class B, Class C, or Class D airspace, or within the lateral boundaries of the surface area of Class E airspace designated for an airport, are not permitted unless that person has prior authorization from air traffic control (ATC) (§107.41). Information concerning the current authorization process is available at faa.gov/uas/. The remote PIC must understand airspace classifications and requirements. Failure to do so could be contrary to part 107 regulations and may potentially have an adverse effect on the safety of operations. Small UAS operating under part 107 may not be subject to part 91 requirements, because the equipage and communications requirements outlined in part 91 were designed to provide safety and efficiency in the National Airspace System (NAS). ATC authorizations may depend on operational parameters similar to those found in part 91. The FAA has the authority to approve or deny aircraft operations based on traffic density, controller workload, communication issues, or any other type of operation that could potentially impact the safe and expeditious flow of air traffic in that airspace.

[AC 107-2]

Chapter 3 Ground Instruction Requirement

9. Unless authorized by ATC and issued in NOTAM, what maximum altitude may a pilot expect a sUAS aircraft to be operated at?

The altitude of the sUAS cannot be higher than 400 feet above ground level, unless the sUAS:

(1) Is flown within a 400-foot radius of a structure; and

(2) Does not fly higher than 400 feet above the structure's immediate uppermost limit.

[14 CFR 107.51]

10. What should a pilot should know with regard to sUAS operating during night hours?

sUAS may be operated at night as long as they have a lighted anticollision lighting visible for at least 3 SM that has a flash rate sufficient to avoid a collision. The remote PIC may reduce the intensity of, but may not extinguish, the anticollision lighting if they determine that, because of operating conditions, it would be in the interest of safety to do so.

[14 CFR 107.29]

I. Weather Reports, Forecasts and Charts

1. How are the following reported in METARs?

Visibilities: Statute or nautical?

Statute

Cloud heights: AGL or MSL?

AGL

Wind directions: True or magnetic north?

True north

Wind speeds: Knots or miles per hour?

Knots

[FAA-H-8083-28]

Chapter 3 **Ground Instruction Requirement**

2. Are the cloud bases and tops in PIREPs expressed in MSL or AGL?

Cloud tops are reported in MSL. The pilot reports MSL altitudes from the altimeter when making the report.

[FAA-H-8083-28]

3. What is a terminal aerodrome forecast (TAF)?

A terminal aerodome forecast is a concise statement of the expected meteorological conditions significant to aviation for a specified time period, within a 5 SM radius from the center of an airport's runway complex (terminal). TAFs use the same weather code found in METAR weather reports, in the following format:

a. *Type of reports*—a routine forecast (TAF), an amended forecast (TAF AMD), or a corrected forecast (TAF COR).

b. *ICAO station identifier*—4-letter station identifiers.

c. *Date and time of origin*—the date/time of forecast follows the terminal's location identifier and shows the day of the month in two digits, and the time in which the forecast is completed and ready for transmission in four digits, appended with a Z to denote UTC. Example: 061737Z—the TAF was issued on the 6th day of the month at 1737 UTC.

d. *Valid period date and time*—The first two digits are the day of the month for the start of the TAF, followed by two digits that indicate the starting hour (UTC). The next two digits indicate the day of the month for the end of the TAF, and the last two digits are the ending hour (UTC) of the valid period. Scheduled 24- and 30-hour TAFs are issued four (4) times per day, at 0000, 0600, 1200, and 1800Z. Example: A 00Z TAF issued on the 9th of the month and valid for 24 hours would have a valid period of 0900/0924.

e. *Forecasts*—wind, visibility, significant and vicinity weather, cloud and vertical obscuration, non-convective low-level wind shear, forecast change indicators (FM, TEMPO and PROB).

[FAA-H-8083-28]

Chapter 3 **Ground Instruction Requirement**

4. What is a Graphical Forecast for Aviation (GFA)?

The Graphical Forecasts for Aviation (GFA) website is intended to provide the necessary aviation weather information to give users a complete picture of the weather that may affect flight in the continental United States (CONUS). The website includes observational data, forecasts, and warnings that can be viewed from 14 hours in the past to 15 hours in the future, including thunderstorms, clouds, flight category, precipitation, icing, turbulence, and wind. Hourly model data and forecasts, including information on clouds, flight category, precipitation, icing, turbulence, wind, and graphical output from the National Weather Service's (NWS) National Digital Forecast Data (NDFD) are available. Wind, icing, and turbulence forecasts are available in 3,000-foot increments from the surface up to 30,000 feet MSL, and in 6,000-foot increments from 30,000 feet MSL to 48,000 feet MSL. Turbulence forecasts are also broken into low (below 18,000 feet MSL) and high (at or above 18,000 feet MSL) graphics. A maximum icing graphic and maximum wind velocity graphic (regardless of altitude) are also available.

The GFA interactive web tool can be viewed at aviationweather.gov/gfa.

[AIM 7-1-4]

5. What type of aviation forecasts are available in the Forecast section of the GFA?

The Forecast section provides gridded displays of various weather parameters as well as NWS textual weather observations, forecasts, and warnings out to 18 hours. Icing, turbulence, and wind gridded products are three-dimensional. Other gridded products are two-dimensional and may represent a composite of a three-dimensional weather phenomenon or a surface weather variable, such as horizontal visibility.

The Forecast section of the GFA provides the following:
a. Ceiling & visibility (CIG/VIS)
b. Clouds
c. Precipitation/weather (PCPN/WX)
d. Thunderstorm (TS)
e. Temperature

Chapter 3 **Ground Instruction Requirement**

   f. Winds
   g. Turbulence
   h. Icing

[AIM 7-1-4, AWC]

6. What valuable information can be determined from winds and temperatures aloft forecasts?

Most favorable altitude—based on winds and direction of flight.

Areas of possible icing—by noting air temperatures of +2° to −20°C.

Temperature inversions.

Turbulence—by observing abrupt changes in wind direction and speed at different altitudes.

[FAA-H-8083-28]

7. What is an AIRMET?

AIRMETs (WAs) are advisories of significant weather phenomena but describe conditions at intensities lower than those which require the issuance of SIGMETs. AIRMETs are intended for dissemination to all pilots in the preflight and en route phase of flight to enhance safety. AIRMET information is available in two formats: text bulletins (WA) and graphics (G-AIRMET) and are issued on a scheduled basis every 6 hours beginning at 0245 UTC. Unscheduled updates and corrections are issued as necessary. AIRMETs contain details about IFR, extensive mountain obscuration, turbulence, strong surface winds, icing, and freezing levels.

[AIM 7-1-6]

8. What are the different types of AIRMETs?

The three types of AIRMETs are Sierra, Tango, and Zulu:

   a. AIRMET Sierra describes IFR conditions and/or extensive mountain obscurations.

   b. AIRMET Tango describes moderate turbulence, sustained surface winds of 30 knots or greater, and/or nonconvective low-level wind shear.

(continued)

Chapter 3 Ground Instruction Requirement

c. AIRMET Zulu describes moderate icing and provides freezing level heights.

[AIM 7-1-6]

9. What is a SIGMET?

SIGMETs (Significant Meteorological Advisory) advise of weather potentially hazardous to all aircraft:

a. Severe icing not associated with a thunderstorm.

b. Severe or extreme turbulence or clear air turbulence (CAT) not associated with thunderstorms.

c. Widespread sand, dust storms or volcanic ash lowering visibilities to less than 3 miles.

d. Volcanic ash.

[FAA-H-8083-28]

10. What is a convective SIGMET?

A convective SIGMET (WST) implies severe or greater turbulence, severe icing and low-level wind shear. It may be issued for any convective situation that the forecaster feels is hazardous to all categories of aircraft. Convective SIGMET bulletins are issued for the Eastern (E), Central (C) and Western (W) United States (convective SIGMETs are not issued for Alaska or Hawaii). Bulletins are issued hourly at H+55. Special bulletins are issued at any time as required and updated at H+55. The text of the bulletin consists of either an observation and a forecast, or just a forecast, which is valid for up to 2 hours.

a. Severe thunderstorm due to:
- Surface winds greater than or equal to 50 knots
- Hail at the surface greater than or equal to ¾ inches in diameter
- Tornadoes

b. Embedded thunderstorms

c. A line of thunderstorms

d. Thunderstorms producing greater than or equal to heavy precipitation that affects 40 percent or more of an area at least 3,000 square miles.

[AIM 7-1-6]

J. Aerodynamics

1. For what two reasons is load factor important to pilots?

a. Because of the obviously dangerous overload that is possible for a pilot to impose on the aircraft structure.

b. Because an increased load factor increases the stalling speed and makes stalls possible at seemingly safe flight speeds.

[FAA-H-8083-3]

2. What situations may result in load factors reaching the maximum or being exceeded?

Level turns—The load factor increases at a terrific rate after a bank has reached 45° or 50°. The load factor in a 60°-bank turn is 2 Gs. The load factor in a 80°-bank turn is 5.76 Gs. The wing must produce lift equal to these load factors if altitude is to be maintained.

Turbulence—Severe vertical gusts cause a sudden increase in angle of attack, resulting in large loads which are resisted by the inertia of the airplane.

Speed—The amount of excess load that can be imposed upon the wing depends on how fast the airplane is flying. At speeds below maneuvering speed, the airplane will stall before the load factor can become excessive. At speeds above maneuvering speed, the limit load factor for which an airplane is stressed can be exceeded by abrupt or excessive application of the controls or by strong turbulence.

[FAA-H-8083-3]

3. What effect does an increase in load factor have on stalling speed?

As load factor increases, stalling speed increases. Load factor increases when an airplane follows a curved flight path, turns, pulls out from a dive, or a sudden or excessive application of back pressure is applied on the control wheel. Consequently, the stalling speed will also increase.

[FAA-H-8083-3]

Chapter 3 **Ground Instruction Requirement**

4. What causes an airplane to stall?

An airplane stalls when the critical angle of attack has been exceeded. When the angle of attack increases to approximately 18° to 20°, the air can no longer flow smoothly over the top wing surface. Because the airflow cannot make such great change in direction so quickly, it becomes impossible for the air to follow the contour of the wing. This is the stalling or critical angle of attack. This can occur at any airspeed, in any attitude, with any power setting.

[FAA-H-8083-3]

5. What major problems can be caused by ground effect?

During landing, at a height of approximately one-tenth of a wing span above the surface, drag may be 40 percent less than when the airplane is operating out of ground effect. Therefore, any excess speed during the landing phase may result in a significant float distance. In such cases, if care is not exercised by the pilot, they may run out of runway and options at the same time.

During takeoff, due to the reduced drag in ground effect, the aircraft may seem capable of takeoff well below the recommended speed. However, as the airplane rises out of ground effect with a deficiency of speed, the greater induced drag may result in very marginal climb performance, or the inability of the airplane to fly at all. In extreme conditions, such as high temperature, high gross weight, and high density altitude, the airplane may become airborne initially with a deficiency of speed and then settle back to the runway.

[FAA-H-8083-3]

6. What is loss of control (LOC)?

A loss of control (LOC) accident involves an unintended departure of an aircraft from controlled flight. LOC can happen because the aircraft enters a flight regime that is outside its normal flight envelope and may quickly develop into a stall or spin. It can introduce an element of surprise for the pilot. Contributing factors may include: poor judgment and/or aeronautical decision making; failure to recognize an aerodynamic stall or spin and execute corrective action; intentional regulatory non-compliance; low

Chapter 3 Ground Instruction Requirement

pilot time in aircraft make and model; lack of piloting ability, experience, and proficiency; failure to maintain airspeed; failure to follow procedure; or the use of over-the-counter drugs that impact pilot performance. Loss of control is the number one cause of accidents.

[FAA-H-8083-3]

7. Define *loss of control inflight* (LOC-I) and describe several situations that might increase the risk of an LOC-I accident occurring.

LOC-I is defined as a significant deviation of an aircraft from the intended flight path and it often results from an airplane upset. Maneuvering is the most common phase of flight for LOC-I accidents to occur; however, LOC-I accidents occur in all phases of flight. Situations that increase the risk of this include uncoordinated flight, equipment malfunctions, pilot complacency, distraction, turbulence, and poor risk management, such as attempting to fly in IMC when the pilot is not qualified or proficient in it.

[FAA-H-8083-3]

8. What is upset recovery, and when do pilots use upset recovery techniques?

Some pilots have failed to prevent airplanes from entering a fully developed upset and have not been able to properly recover from such events, resulting in a LOC-I. An upset is when an airplane in flight unintentionally exceeds the parameters normally experienced in line operations or training: pitch attitude greater than 25 degrees nose up; pitch attitude greater than 10 degrees nose down; bank angle greater than 45 degrees; or flying at airspeeds inappropriate for the conditions. In addition to stall training, Upset Prevention and Recovery Training (UPRT) is an essential training element to reduce loss of control events or enable recovery to normal flight if they occur. UPRT curriculum focuses on preventing upsets rather than waiting to recover from one. The focus on prevention is a significant shift from previous upset or unusual attitude training, which primarily focused on recovering from a fully developed upset. Prevention training prepares pilots to avoid incidents, while recovery training intends to avoid an accident if an upset occurs.

[FAA-H-8083-3]

Chapter 3   Ground Instruction Requirement

K. Weight and Balance

1. What basic equation is used in all weight and balance problems to find the center of gravity location of an airplane and/or its components?

Weight × Arm = Moment

By rearrangement of this equation:

Weight = Moment/Arm

Arm (CG) = (Total) Moment/(Total) Weight

With any two known values, the third value can be found.

Remember: W A M (*W*eight × *A*rm = *M*oment)

2. Where is a pilot supposed to find weight and balance information for their aircraft?

A pilot must properly determine the aircraft is being operated within weight and balance limitations as established by the manufacturer or in accordance with any subsequent STC changes. Most manufacturers include a weight and balance with the certification of the aircraft, many times in the airplane flight manual. As the aircraft experience equipment changes over time, these are commonly updated. Most aircraft operators consider a current weight and balance to be required documentation to have onboard the aircraft and the pilot can typically find this in the aircraft flight manuals and/or supplements. While it may be of note that 14 CFR Part 23 says that a W&B must be furnished by the manufacturer it does not actually state that that it must be in the aircraft. There are several FARs, especially 14 CFR §91.103, preflight action, that require you to consult the W&B information before flight. This does not specifically require the pilot to have a copy of the current W&B in the aircraft when it is in flow but a pilot is required to have determined that the flight will be conducted within weight and balance limitations. As a practical matter most pilots keep a copy of the current weight and balance in the aircraft. This fact does allow for a pilot to utilize digital copies of the weight and balance or an EFB based weight and balance calculation with appropriate data. If an aircraft was certificated with an approved flight manual it may be a component of that manual (and is in most modern aircraft) that then does cause the weight and balance information to then become a required document.

[14 CFR 91.203, FAA-H-8083-1, FAA-H-8083-25, 14 CFR 23.1589]

3. What is one major danger of a pilot utilizing weight and balance software on a computer or an EFB device?

Many standard aircraft profiles included in software are not customized to specific aircraft weight and balance stations, aircraft weights, or loading parameters. Using a standard profile that is not updated to the specific information for the aircraft to be flown based on current weight and balance parameters may lead to a pilot operating outside of the prescribed weight and balance operations limitations for the aircraft.

4. What performance characteristics will be adversely affected when an aircraft has been overloaded?

a. Higher takeoff speed.
b. Longer takeoff run.
c. Reduced rate and angle of climb.
d. Lower maximum altitude.
e. Shorter range.
f. Reduced cruising speed.
g. Reduced maneuverability.
h. Higher stall speed.
i. Higher landing speed.
j. Longer landing roll.
k. Excessive weight on the nosewheel.

[FAA-H-8083-1]

5. What effect does a forward center of gravity have on an aircraft's flight characteristics?

Higher stall speed—stalling angle of attack is reached at a higher speed due to increased wing loading.

Slower cruise speed—increased drag; greater angle of attack is required to maintain altitude.

More stable—the center of gravity is farther forward from the center of pressure which increases longitudinal stability.

(continued)

Chapter 3 **Ground Instruction Requirement**

Greater back elevator pressure required—longer takeoff roll; higher approach speeds and problems with landing flare.

[FAA-H-8083-3]

6. What effect does a rearward center of gravity have on an aircraft's flight characteristics?

Lower stall speed—less wing loading.

Higher cruise speed—reduced drag; smaller angle of attack is required to maintain altitude.

Less stable—stall and spin recovery more difficult; the center of gravity is closer to the center of pressure, causing longitudinal instability.

[FAA-H-8083-3]

7. What is the weight of aircraft fuel and oil?

Aircraft fuel weighs 6 pounds per gallon. Aircraft oil weighs 7.5 pounds per gallon.

[FAA-H-8083-25]

L. Aircraft Performance

1. How does weight affect takeoff and landing performance?

Increased gross weight can have a significant effect on takeoff performance:

a. Higher liftoff speed;
b. Greater mass to accelerate (slow acceleration);
c. Increased retarding force (drag and ground friction); and
d. Longer takeoff distance.

The effect of gross weight on landing distance is that the airplane will require a greater speed to support the airplane at the landing angle of attack and lift coefficient resulting in an increased landing distance.

[FAA-H-8083-3]

Chapter 3 Ground Instruction Requirement

2. **How does air density affect takeoff and landing performance?**

   An increase in density altitude (decrease in air density) can also have the following effects on takeoff performance:
   a. Greater takeoff speed required;
   b. Decreased thrust and reduced acceleration;
   c. Longer takeoff ground roll; and
   d. Decreased climb rate.

   An increase in density altitude (decrease in air density) will increase the landing ground speed but will not alter the net retarding force. Thus, the airplane will land at the same indicated airspeed as normal but because of reduced air density the true airspeed will be greater. This will result in a longer minimum landing distance.

   [FAA-H-8083-3]

3. **Know the following speeds for your airplane:**

   V_S: _____ Stall speed of the aircraft in clean configuration.

   V_{S0}: _____ Stall speed in landing configuration; the calibrated power-off stalling speed or the minimum steady flight speed at which the airplane is controllable in the landing configuration.

   V_{S1}: _____ Stall speed clean or in specified configuration; the calibrated power-off stalling speed or the minimum steady speed at which the airplane is controllable in a specified configuration.

   V_Y: _____ Best rate-of-climb speed; the calibrated airspeed at which the airplane will obtain the maximum increase in altitude per unit of time. This best rate-of-climb speed normally decreases slightly with altitude.

   V_X: _____ Best angle-of-climb speed; the calibrated airspeed at which the airplane will obtain the highest altitude in a given horizontal distance. This best angle-of-climb speed normally increases with altitude.

   V_{LE}: _____ Maximum landing gear extension speed; the maximum calibrated airspeed at which the airplane can be safely flown with the landing gear extended. This is a problem involving stability and controllability.

   (continued)

Chapter 3   Ground Instruction Requirement

V_{LO}: _____ Maximum landing gear operating speed; the maximum calibrated airspeed at which the landing gear can be safely extended or retracted. This is a problem involving the airloads imposed on the operating mechanism during extension or retraction of the gear.

V_{FE}: _____ Maximum flap extension speed; the highest calibrated airspeed permissible with the wing flaps in a prescribed extended position. This is a problem involving the airloads imposed on the structure of the flaps.

V_A: _____ Maneuvering speed; the calibrated design maneuvering airspeed. This is the maximum speed at which the limit load can be imposed (either by gusts or full deflection of the control surfaces) without causing structural damage.

V_H: _____ Maximum speed in level flight with maximum continuous power.

V_{NO}: _____ Normal operating speed; the maximum calibrated airspeed for normal operation or the maximum structural cruise speed. This is the speed above which exceeding the limit load factor may cause permanent deformation of the airplane structure.

V_{NE}: _____ Never exceed speed; the calibrated airspeed which should never be exceeded. If flight is attempted above this speed, structural damage or structural failure may result.

4. **The following questions are designed to provide the pilot with a general review of the basic information they should know about their specific airplane before taking a flight check or review.**

   a. What is the normal climb-out speed?
   b. What is the normal approach-to-land speed?
   c. What is red-line speed?
   d. What engine-out glide speed will give you maximum range?
   e. What is the make and horsepower of the engine?
   f. How many usable gallons of fuel can you carry?
   g. Where are the fuel tanks located and what are their capacities?
   h. What is the octane rating of the fuel used by your aircraft?
   i. How do you drain the fuel sumps?

j. What are the minimum and maximum oil capacities?
k. What weight of oil is being used?
l. What is the maximum oil temperature and pressure?
m. Is the landing gear fixed, manual, hydraulic or electric? If retractable, what is the backup system for lowering the gear?
n. What is the maximum demonstrated crosswind component for the aircraft?
o. How many people will this aircraft carry safely with a full fuel load?
p. What is the maximum allowable weight the aircraft can carry with baggage in the baggage compartment?
q. What takeoff distance is required if a takeoff were made from a sea-level pressure altitude?
r. What is your maximum allowable useful load?
s. Solve a weight and balance problem for the flight you plan to make with one passenger at 170 pounds.
   - Does your load fall within the weight and balance envelope?
   - What is the final gross weight?
   - How much fuel can be carried?
   - How much baggage can be carried with full fuel?
t. Know the function of the various types of antennae on your aircraft.

M. Navigation

1. **What type of aeronautical charts are available for use in VFR navigation?**

   a. *Sectional Charts*—designed for visual navigation of slow to medium speed aircraft. One inch equals 6.86 nautical miles. They are revised semiannually, except most Alaskan charts which are revised annually.

   b. *VFR Terminal Area Charts (TAC)*—TACs depict the Class B airspace. While similar to sectional charts, TACs have more detail because the scale is larger. One inch equals 3.43 nautical miles. Charts are revised semiannually, except in Puerto Rico and the Virgin Islands where they are revised annually.

(continued)

Chapter 3 **Ground Instruction Requirement**

    c. *VFR Flyway Planning Charts*—This chart is printed on the reverse side of selected TAC charts. The coverage is the same as the associated TAC. They depict flight paths and altitudes recommended for use to bypass high traffic areas.

Note: World Aeronautical Charts (WAC) are no longer available.

[AIM 9-1-4]

2. What is *magnetic variation*?

Magnetic variation is the error induced by the difference in location of true north and magnetic north. It is expressed in east or west variation.

[FAA-H-8083-25]

3. How do you convert a true direction to a magnetic direction?

To convert from TRUE (measured from the meridians on the chart) to MAGNETIC, note the variation shown by the nearest isogonic line. If variation is west, add; if east, subtract.

Remember: East is Least (Subtract)
                 West is Best (Add)

[FAA-H-8083-25]

4. What is *magnetic deviation*?

Because of magnetic influences within the airplane itself (electrical circuits, radios, lights, tools, engine, magnetized metal parts, etc.) the compass needle is frequently deflected from its normal reading. This deflection is called deviation. Deviation is different for each airplane, and also varies for different headings of the same airplane. The deviation value may be found on a deviation card located in the airplane.

[FAA-H-8083-25]

N. Cross-Country Flying

1. Flight log example, VFR flight plan:

Careful preflight planning is extremely important. A wise pilot ensures a successful cross-country flight by getting a good weather briefing and completing a flight log before flight.

a. Get a weather briefing from a Flight Service Station. Write it down.
b. Draw course lines and mark checkpoints on the chart.
c. Enter checkpoints on the log.
d. Enter NAVAIDs on the log.
e. Enter VOR courses on the log.
f. Enter altitude on the log.
g. Enter the wind (direction/speed) and temperature on the log.
h. Measure the true course on the chart and enter it on the log.
i. Compute the true airspeed and enter it on the log.
j. Compute the WCA and GS and enter them on the log.
k. Determine variation from chart and enter it on the log.
l. Determine deviation from compass correction card and enter it on the log.
m. Measure distances on the chart and enter them on the log.
n. Figure ETE and ETA and enter them on the log.
o. Calculate fuel burn and usage; enter them on the log.
p. Compute weight and balance.
q. Compute takeoff and landing performance.
r. Complete a Flight Plan form.
s. File a Flight Plan with flight service.

Chapter 3 **Ground Instruction Requirement**

2. **Diversion to alternate/lost procedures:**

   What actions should be taken if you become disoriented or lost on a cross-country flight?

   Condition I: plenty of fuel and weather conditions good.

   a. Straighten up and fly right. Fly a specific heading in a direction you believe to be correct (or circle, if unsure); don't wander aimlessly.

   b. If you have been flying a steady compass heading and keeping a relatively accurate navigation log, it's not likely you will have a problem locating your position.

   c. If several VORs are within reception distance, use them for a cross-bearing to determine position (even a single VOR can be enormous help in narrowing down your possible position); or, fly to the station—there's no doubt where you are then.

   d. Use knowledge of your last known position, elapsed time, approximate wind direction and ground speed, to establish how far you may have traveled since your last checkpoint.

   e. Use this distance as a radius and draw a semicircle ahead of your last known position on chart. For example, you estimate your ground speed at 120 knots. If you have been flying 20 minutes since your last checkpoint, then the no-wind radius of your semicircle is 40 miles projected along the direction of your estimated track.

   f. If still unsure of your position, loosen up the eyeballs and start some first-class pilotage. Look for something big. Don't concern yourself with the minute or trivial at this point. Often, there will be linear features such as rivers, mountain ranges, or prominent highways and railroads that are easy to identify. You can use them simply as references for orientation purposes and thus find them of great value in fixing your approximate position.

   Condition II: low on fuel; weather deteriorating; inadequate experience; darkness imminent; and/or equipment malfunctioning.

   Get it on the ground! Most accidents are the product of mistakes which have multiplied over a period of time and getting lost is no exception: don't push your luck. It may well be that in doing so,

Chapter 3 **Ground Instruction Requirement**

you have added the final mistake which will add another figure to the accident statistics. If terrain or other conditions make landing impossible at the moment, don't waste time, for it is of the essence: don't search for the perfect field—anything usable will do. Remember, most people on the ground know where they are, and you know that you do not.

3. If it becomes apparent that you cannot locate your position, what action is recommended at this point?

The FAA recommends the use of the 4 Cs:

a. *Climb*—The higher altitude allows better communication capability as well as better visual range for identification of landmarks.

b. *Communicate*—Use the system. Use 121.5 MHz if no other frequency produced results. It is guarded by flight service's, control towers, military towers, approach control facilities, and Air Route Traffic Control Centers.

c. *Confess*—Once communications are established, let them know your problem.

d. *Comply*—Follow instructions.

4. While en route on a cross-country flight, weather has deteriorated and it becomes necessary to divert to an alternate airport. What is the recommended procedure?

a. Mark your present position on the chart. It is also advisable to write the current time next to this mark.

b. Establish a general direction to the alternate and turn to it immediately.

c. As time permits, determine distance, ground speed, and estimated time en route to the alternate.

O. Radio Communications

1. What is the universal VHF emergency frequency?

121.5 MHz; this frequency is guarded by military towers, most civil towers, flight service stations, and radar facilities.

[AIM 6-3-1]

Chapter 3 **Ground Instruction Requirement**

2. If operating into an airport without an operating control tower, flight service or UNICOM, what procedure should be followed?

A pilot should monitor the multicom frequency of 122.9 when approaching the airport and broadcast intentions when approximately five miles out. Multicom is a mobile service not open to public use, used to provide communications essential to conduct the activities being performed by or directed from private aircraft.

[AIM 4-1-9]

3. What are the standard Flight Service Station frequencies?

122.0 MHz for the flight service common frequency or via charted remote communication outlet (RCO) frequencies as well as any local frequencies listed within the *Chart Supplement*.

[AIM 4-2-14]

4. What is *Local Airport Advisory* service?

Certain flight service's provide Local Airport Advisory (LAA) service to pilots when an flight service is physically located on an airport that doesn't have a control tower or where the tower is operated on a part-time basis. The CTAF (usually 123.6) for flight service's that provide this service will be disseminated in appropriate aeronautical publications. A CTAF flight service provides wind direction and speed, NOTAMs, taxi routes, traffic pattern information, and instrument approach procedures. The information is advisory in nature and does not constitute an ATC clearance.

[AIM 4-1-9]

5. What should a pilot know about intercept procedures if they are intercepted while flying?

If the U.S. military intercepts an aircraft and flares are dispensed in the area of that aircraft, aviators will pay strict attention, contact air traffic control immediately on the local frequency or on VHF guard 121.5 and follow the intercept's visual ICAO signals. Be advised that noncompliance may result in the use of force. If a pilot is flying with flight following and in contact with ATC, ATC may advise the pilot of the intercept and instructions.

[AIM 5-6-2]

P. Federal Aviation Regulations Part 91

1. If an in-flight emergency requires immediate action by the pilot, what authority and responsibilities do they have?

   a. The pilot-in-command is directly responsible for and is the final authority as to the operation of an aircraft.

   b. The pilot-in-command may deviate from any regulation to the extent necessary in dealing with the emergency.

   c. A pilot-in-command who deviates from a regulation to meet an emergency must send a written report to the FAA if so requested.

   [14 CFR 91.3]

2. Concerning a flight in the local area, is any preflight action required, and if so, what must it consist of?

Yes. Pilots must familiarize themselves with all available information concerning that flight, including runway lengths at airports of intended use, and takeoff and landing distance data under existing conditions.

[14 CFR 91.103]

3. Preflight action as required by regulation for all flights away from the vicinity of the departure airport shall include a review of what specific information?

For a flight under IFR or a flight not in the vicinity of an airport:

   a. Weather reports and forecasts.

   b. Fuel requirements.

   c. Alternatives available if the planned flight cannot be completed.

   d. Any known traffic delays of which the pilot-in-command has been advised by ATC.

   e. Runway lengths of intended use.

   f. Takeoff and landing distance data.

   [14 CFR 91.103]

Chapter 3 Ground Instruction Requirement

4. Which persons on board an aircraft are required to use seatbelts and when?

During takeoff and landing, each person on board an aircraft must occupy a seat or berth with a safety belt and shoulder harness, if installed, properly secured about them. However, a person who has not reached his or her second birthday may be held by an adult who is occupying a seat or a berth, and a person on board for the purpose of engaging in sport parachuting may use the floor of the aircraft as a seat.

[14 CFR 91.107]

5. If operating an aircraft in close proximity to another, such as formation flight, what regulations apply?

a. No person may operate an aircraft so close to another aircraft as to create a collision hazard.

b. No person may operate an aircraft in formation flight except by arrangement with the pilot-in-command of each aircraft in the formation.

c. No person may operate an aircraft carrying passengers for hire in formation flight.

[14 CFR 91.111]

6. What is the order of right-of-way as applied to the different categories of aircraft?

a. A balloon has the right-of-way over any other category of aircraft.

b. A glider has the right-of way over an airship, powered parachute, weight-shift control aircraft, airplane, or rotorcraft.

c. An airship has the right-of-way over a powered parachute, weight-shift control aircraft, airplane, or rotorcraft.

Aircraft towing or refueling other aircraft have the right-of-way over all other engine-driven aircraft.

[14 CFR 91.113]

Chapter 3 Ground Instruction Requirement

7. When would an aircraft have the right-of-way over all other air traffic?

An aircraft in distress has the right-of-way over all other air traffic.

[14 CFR 91.113]

8. State the required action for each of the aircraft confrontations: converging, approaching head-on, overtaking.

Converging: aircraft on right has the right-of-way if same category. Otherwise, see Question 8.

Approaching head-on: both aircraft shall alter course to right.

Overtaking: aircraft being overtaken has the right-of-way; pilot of the overtaking aircraft shall alter course to the right.

[14 CFR 91.113]

9. What right-of-way rules apply when two or more aircraft are approaching an airport for the purpose of landing?

Aircraft on final approach to land or while landing have the right-of-way over aircraft in flight or operating on the surface, except that they shall not take advantage of this rule to force an aircraft off the runway surface which has already landed and is attempting to make way for an aircraft on final approach. When two or more aircraft are approaching an airport for the purpose of landing, the aircraft at the lower altitude has the right-of-way, but it shall not take advantage of this rule to cut in front of another which is on final approach to land or to overtake that aircraft.

[14 CFR 91.113, AC 90-66]

10. What advice does the FAA give regarding arriving in traffic pattern operations at non-towered airports?

Arriving aircraft should enter the airport's traffic pattern at traffic pattern altitude and avoid straight-in approaches for landing to mitigate the risk of a midair collision.

Prior to entering the traffic pattern at an airport without an operating control tower, aircraft should avoid the flow of traffic until established on the entry leg. For example, the pilot can check wind and landing direction indicators while at an altitude above

Chapter 3 **Ground Instruction Requirement**

the traffic pattern, or by monitoring the communications of other traffic that communicate the runway in use, especially at airports with more than one runway. When the runway in use and proper traffic pattern direction have been determined, the pilot should then proceed to a point well clear of the pattern before descending to and entering at pattern altitude.

Arriving aircraft should be at traffic pattern altitude and allow for sufficient time to view the entire traffic pattern before entering. Entries into traffic patterns while descending may create collision hazards and should be avoided. Entry to the downwind leg should be at a 45-degree angle abeam the midpoint of the runway to be used for landing. Aircraft should always enter the pattern at pattern altitude, especially when flying over midfield and entering the downwind directly.

[AC 90-66]

11. How should a pilot plan to exit a traffic pattern at a non-towered airport?

When departing the traffic pattern, airplanes should continue straight out or exit with a 45-degree left turn (right turn for right traffic pattern) beyond the departure end of the runway after reaching pattern altitude. Pilots need to be aware of any traffic entering the traffic pattern prior to commencing a turn.

[AC 90-66]

12. Who has right of way when approaching an airport: A pilot established in the traffic pattern or one approaching using an approach procedure in VFR conditions from a straight-in approach?

To mitigate the risk of a midair collision at a non-towered airport in other than instrument conditions, the FAA does not recommend that the pilot execute a straight-in approach for landing when other aircraft are in the traffic pattern. The straight-in approach may cause a conflict with aircraft in the traffic pattern and on base to final and increase the risk of a midair collision.

Chapter 3 **Ground Instruction Requirement**

The FAA discourages VFR straight-in approaches to landings due to increased risk of a midair collision. However, if a pilot chooses to execute a straight-in approach for landing without entering the airport traffic pattern, the pilot should self-announce their position on the designated CTAF between 8 and approximately 10 miles from the airport and coordinate their straight-in approach and landing with other airport traffic. Pilots choosing to execute a straight-in approach do not have a particular priority over other aircraft in the traffic pattern and must comply with the provisions of §91.113(g).

13. Unless otherwise authorized or required by ATC, what is the maximum indicated airspeed at which a person may operate an aircraft below 10,000 feet MSL?

No person may operate an aircraft below 10,000 feet MSL at an indicated airspeed of more than 250 knots (288 mph).

[14 CFR 91.117]

14. What is the minimum safe altitude that an aircraft may be operated over a congested area of a city?

Except when necessary for takeoff or landing, no person may operate an aircraft over a congested area of a city, town, or settlement, or over any open-air assembly of persons, below an altitude of 1,000 feet above the highest obstacle within a horizontal radius of 2,000 feet of the aircraft.

[14 CFR 91.119]

15. In areas other than congested areas, what minimum safe altitudes shall be used?

Except when necessary for takeoff or landing, an aircraft shall be operated no lower than 500 feet above the surface, except over open water or sparsely populated areas. In those cases, the aircraft may not be operated closer than 500 feet to any person, vessel, vehicle or structure.

[14 CFR 91.119]

Chapter 3 Ground Instruction Requirement

16. When flying below 18,000 feet MSL, cruising altitude must be maintained by reference to an altimeter set using what procedure?

When the barometric pressure is 31.00 inHg or less, each person operating an aircraft shall maintain the cruising altitude or flight level of that aircraft, as the case may be, by reference to an altimeter set to the current reported altimeter setting of a station along the route and within 100 nautical miles of the aircraft. If there is no station within this area, the current reported altimeter setting of an available station may be used. If the barometric pressure exceeds 31.00 inHg, consult the *Aeronautical Information Manual* for correct procedures.

[14 CFR 91.121]

17. If an altimeter setting is not available before flight, what procedure should be used?

Use the same procedure as in the case of an aircraft not equipped with a radio: the elevation of the departure airport or an appropriate altimeter setting available before departure should be used.

[14 CFR 91.121]

18. When may a pilot intentionally deviate from an ATC clearance or instruction?

No pilot may deviate from an ATC clearance unless an amended clearance has been obtained, an emergency exists, or if the pilot is acting in response to a traffic and collision avoidance system resolution advisory or for the purposes of an in-flight emergency requiring immediate action.

[14 CFR 91.123]

19. As pilot-in-command, what action, if any, is required of you if you deviate from an ATC instruction and priority is given?

Two actions are required of you as PIC:
   a. Each pilot-in-command who, in an emergency, deviates from an ATC clearance or instruction shall notify ATC of that deviation as soon as possible (in-the-air responsibility).

b. Each pilot-in-command who is given priority by ATC in an emergency shall submit a detailed report of that emergency within 48 hours to the manager of that ATC facility, if requested by ATC (on-the-ground responsibility).

[14 CFR 91.123]

20. **In the event of radio failure while operating at tower controlled airports within Class B, C, or D airspace, what are the different types and meanings of light gun signals you might receive from an ATC tower?**

Light	On Ground	In Air
Steady green	Cleared for takeoff	Cleared to land
Flashing green	Cleared to taxi	Return for landing
Steady red	Stop	Yield, continue circling
Flashing red	Taxi clear of runway	Unsafe, do not land
Flashing white	Return to start	Not used
Alternating red/green	Exercise extreme caution	Exercise extreme caution

[14 CFR 91.125]

21. **What general rules apply concerning traffic pattern operations at non-tower airports within Class E or G airspace?**

Each person operating an aircraft to or from an airport without an operating control tower shall:

a. In the case of an airplane approaching to land, make all turns of that airplane to the left unless the airport displays approved light signals or visual markings indicating that turns should be made to the right, in which case the pilot shall make all turns to the right.

b. In the case of an aircraft departing an airport, comply with any traffic patterns established for that airport in Part 93.

[14 CFR 91.126, 91.127]

Chapter 3   **Ground Instruction Requirement**

22. What procedure should be used when approaching to land on a runway with a visual approach slope indicator?

Aircraft approaching to land on a runway served by a visual approach slope indicator shall maintain an altitude at or above the glide slope until a lower altitude is necessary for a safe landing.

[14 CFR 91.129]

23. What is the fuel requirement for VFR flight at night?

No person may begin a flight in an airplane under VFR conditions unless (considering wind and forecast weather conditions) there is enough fuel to fly to the first point of intended landing and, assuming normal cruising speed, at night, fly after that for at least 45 minutes.

[14 CFR 91.151]

24. What is the fuel requirement for VFR flight during the day?

During the day, you must be able to fly to the first point of intended landing, and assuming normal cruising speed, fly after that for at least 30 minutes.

[14 CFR 91.151]

25. When operating an aircraft under VFR in level cruising flight at an altitude of more than 3,000 feet above the surface, what rules apply concerning specific altitudes flown?

When operating above 3,000 feet AGL but less than 18,000 feet MSL on a *magnetic course* of 0° to 179°, fly at an odd-thousand-foot MSL altitude plus 500 feet. When on a *magnetic course* of 180° to 359°, fly at an even-thousand-foot MSL altitude plus 500 feet.

[14 CFR 91.159]

26. What instruments and equipment are required for VFR day flight?

For VFR flight during the day, the following instruments and equipment are required:

a. Airspeed indicator.
b. Altimeter.
c. Magnetic direction indicator compass.
d. Tachometer for each engine.
e. Oil pressure gauge for each engine.
f. Temperature gauge for each liquid-cooled engine.
g. Oil temperature gauge for each air-cooled engine.
h. Manifold pressure gauge for each altitude engine.
i. Fuel gauge indicating the quantity in each tank.
j. Landing gear position indicator.
k. Flotation gear (if operated for hire over water beyond power-off gliding distance from shore).
l. Safety belts (approved metal-to-metal latching device for each occupant over 2 years old).
m. Shoulder harnesses (for each front seat if aircraft manufactured after 1978).
n. Emergency locator transmitter.

[14 CFR 91.205]

27. What instruments and equipment are required for VFR night flight?

For VFR flight at night, the following instruments and equipment are required:

a. Instruments and equipment required for VFR day flight;
b. Approved position lights (navigation lights);
c. An approved aviation red or aviation white anticollision light system;
d. If the aircraft is operated for hire, one electric landing light;

(continued)

Chapter 3 **Ground Instruction Requirement**

    e. An adequate source of electrical energy for all installed electrical and radio equipment; and

    f. One spare set of fuses, or three spare fuses of each kind required, that are accessible to the pilot in flight.

[14 CFR 91.205]

28. Is an emergency locator transmitter (ELT) required on all aircraft?

Yes. No person may operate a U.S.-registered civil airplane unless there is attached to the airplane an automatic-type emergency locator transmitter that is in operable condition. Several exceptions exist, including the following:

    a. Aircraft engaged in training operations conducted entirely within a 50-nautical-mile radius of the airport from which such local flight operations began.

    b. Aircraft engaged in design and testing.

    c. New aircraft engaged in manufacture, preparation and delivery.

    d. Aircraft engaged in agricultural operations.

[14 CFR 91.207]

29. When must the batteries in an emergency locator transmitter be replaced or recharged, if rechargeable?

Batteries used in ELTs must be replaced (or recharged, if the batteries are rechargeable):

    a. When the transmitter has been in use for more than 1 cumulative hour; or

    b. When 50 percent of their useful life (or, if rechargeable batteries, 50 percent of their useful life of charge), has expired.

[14 CFR 91.207]

30. When must a pilot operate aircraft anticollision lighting?

If equipped, a pilot must operate an aircraft anticollision lighting system at all times when the aircraft is in operation. *Operate* is defined in 14 CFR §1.1 as to "use, cause to use or authorize use of the aircraft for the purpose of air navigation." The FAA has stated that the term *operate* applies to "those acts which impart some physical movement of to the aircraft, or involve manipulation of the controls of the aircraft such as starting or running an aircraft engine." These lights must be visible from 360 degrees of the aircraft when on the ground and in the air. Typically, this is complied with through a rotating beacon on the top or bottom of the aircraft or through strobe lights on each wing of the aircraft.

[14 CFR 61.209]

31. When must the required position lights be on?

Aircraft position lights must be on during operations from sunset to sunrise.

[14 CFR 91.209]

32. What are the regulations concerning use of supplemental oxygen on board an aircraft?

a. At cabin pressure altitudes above 12,500 feet MSL up to and including 14,000 feet MSL: for that part of the flight at those altitudes that is more than 30 minutes, the required minimum flight crew must be provided with and use supplemental oxygen.

b. At cabin pressure altitudes above 14,000 feet MSL up to and including 15,000 feet MSL: for the entire flight time at those altitudes, the required flight crew is provided with and uses supplemental oxygen.

c. At cabin pressure altitudes above 15,000 feet MSL: each occupant is provided with supplemental oxygen.

[14 CFR 91.211]

33. According to regulations, where is aerobatic flight of an aircraft not permitted?

No person may operate an aircraft in aerobatic flight:

a. Over any congested area of city, town, or settlement;

b. Over an open air assembly of persons;

c. Within the lateral boundaries of the surface areas of Class B, Class C, Class D, Class E airspace designated for an airport;

d. Within 4 nautical miles of the center line of a Federal airway;

e. Below an altitude of 1,500 feet above the surface; or

f. When flight visibility is less than 3 statute miles.

[14 CFR 91.303]

Chapter 3 **Ground Instruction Requirement**

34. Define *aerobatic flight*.

Aerobatic flight means an intentional maneuver involving an abrupt change in an aircraft's attitude, an abnormal attitude, or abnormal acceleration, not necessary for normal flight.

[14 CFR 91.303]

35. When are parachutes required on board an aircraft?
   a. Unless each occupant of the aircraft is wearing an approved parachute, no pilot of a civil aircraft carrying any person (other than a crewmember) may execute any intentional maneuver that exceeds:
      - A bank angle of 60° relative to the horizon; or
      - A nose-up or nose-down attitude of 30° relative to the horizon.
   b. The above regulation does not apply to:
      - Flight tests for pilot certification or rating; or
      - Spins and other flight maneuvers required by the regulations for any certificate or rating when given by a flight instructor or ATP instructing in accordance with 14 CFR §61.169.

[14 CFR 91.307]

Q. Airspace

1. What is Class A airspace?

Generally, that airspace from 18,000 feet MSL up to and including FL600, including that airspace overlying the waters within 12 nautical miles of the coast of the 48 contiguous states and Alaska; and designated international airspace beyond 12 nautical miles of the coast of the 48 contiguous states and Alaska within areas of domestic radio navigational signal or ATC radar coverage, and within which domestic procedures are applied.

[AIM 3-2-2]

2. Can a flight under VFR be conducted within Class A airspace?

No. Unless otherwise authorized by ATC, each person operating an aircraft in Class A airspace must operate that aircraft under instrument flight rules (IFR).

[14 CFR 91.135]

Chapter 3 **Ground Instruction Requirement**

3. **What is the minimum pilot certification for operations conducted within Class A airspace?**

   The pilot must be at least a private pilot with an instrument rating.

   [14 CFR 91.135]

4. **What minimum equipment is required for flight operations within Class A airspace?**

   a. A two-way radio capable of communicating with ATC on the frequency assigned.
   b. A Mode C altitude encoding transponder.
   c. Instruments and equipment required for IFR operations.

   [14 CFR 91.135]

5. **How is Class A airspace depicted on navigation charts?**

   Class A airspace is not specifically charted.

   [AIM 3-2-2]

6. **What is the definition of Class B airspace?**

   Generally, that airspace from the surface to 10,000 feet MSL surrounding the nation's busiest airports in terms of IFR operations or passenger enplanements. The configuration of each Class B airspace area is individually tailored and consists of a surface area and two or more layers (some Class B airspace areas resemble upside-down wedding cakes), and is designated to contain all published instrument procedures once an aircraft enters the airspace.

   [AIM 3-2-3]

7. **What minimum pilot certification is required to operate an aircraft within Class B airspace?**

   No person may take off or land a civil aircraft at an airport within a Class B airspace area or operate a civil aircraft within a Class B airspace area unless:

   a. In order to take off or land at an airport within Class B airspace, including the primary airport, a pilot must hold at least a private pilot certificate or be a student or recreational pilot who has

Chapter 3 **Ground Instruction Requirement**

met the requirements of 14 CFR §61.95 (Operations in Class B airspace and at airports located with Class B airspace).

b. Certain Class B airspace areas do not allow student pilot operations to be conducted to or from the primary airport, unless the pilot-in-command holds at least a private pilot certificate (example: Dallas/Fort Worth International).

[14 CFR 91.131]

8. What is the minimum equipment required for operations of an aircraft within Class B airspace?

a. An operable two-way radio capable of communications with ATC on the appropriate frequencies for that area.

b. A Mode C altitude encoding transponder.

c. If IFR, a VOR is also required.

[14 CFR 91.131]

9. Before operating an aircraft into Class B airspace, what basic requirement must be met?

Arriving aircraft must obtain an ATC clearance from the ATC facility having jurisdiction for that area prior to operating an aircraft in that area.

[14 CFR 91.131]

10. What minimum weather conditions are required when conducting VFR flight operations within Class B airspace?

VFR flight operations must be conducted clear of clouds with at least 3 statute miles flight visibility.

[14 CFR 91.155]

11. How is Class B airspace depicted on navigational charts?

Class B airspace is charted on Sectional Charts, IFR En Route Low Altitude Charts, and Terminal Area Charts. A solid shaded blue line depicts the lateral limits of Class B airspace. The base and ceiling of the airspace is shown with one number over another, i.e., 100/25.

[AIM 3-2-3]

Chapter 3 **Ground Instruction Requirement**

12. What basic ATC services are provided to all aircraft operating within Class B airspace?

VFR pilots will be provided sequencing and separation from other aircraft while operating within Class B airspace.

[AIM 3-2-3]

13. It becomes apparent that wake turbulence may be encountered while ATC is providing sequencing and separation services in Class B airspace. Whose responsibility is it to avoid this turbulence?

The pilot-in-command is responsible. These services provided by ATC do not relieve pilots of their responsibilities to see and avoid other traffic operating in basic VFR weather conditions, to adjust their operations and flight path as necessary to preclude serious wake turbulence encounters or to maintain appropriate terrain and obstruction clearance.

[AIM 3-2-3]

14. What is the maximum speed an aircraft may be operated within Class B airspace?

Unless otherwise authorized by the Administrator (or by ATC), no person may operate an aircraft below 10,000 feet MSL at an indicated airspeed of more than 250 knots (288 mph).

[14 CFR 91.117]

15. When operating beneath the lateral limits of Class B airspace, or in a VFR corridor designated through Class B airspace, what maximum speed is authorized?

No person may operate an aircraft in the airspace underlying a Class B airspace area or in a VFR corridor designated through such a Class B airspace area, at an indicated airspeed of more than 200 knots (230 mph).

[14 CFR 91.117]

Chapter 3 **Ground Instruction Requirement**

16. What is Class C airspace?

Generally, that airspace from the surface to 4,000 feet above the airport elevation (charted in MSL) surrounding those airports that have an operational control tower, are serviced by a radar approach control, and that have a certain number of IFR operations or passenger enplanements.

[AIM 3-2-4]

17. What are the basic dimensions of Class C airspace?

Although the configuration of each Class C airspace area is individually tailored, the airspace usually consists of two circles both centered on the primary airport for the Class C airspace. The surface area has a radius of 5 NM. The shelf area has a radius of 10 NM. The airspace of the inner circle extends from the surface up to 4,000 feet above the airport. The airspace area between the 5 and 10 NM rings begin at a height 1,200 feet AGL and extends to the same altitude cap as the surface area. The outer area consists of airspace beginning at 10 NM extending to a radius of 20 NM from the primary airport and extends from the lower limits of radar/radio coverage up to the ceiling of the approach controls delegated airspace.

[AIM 3-2-4]

18. What minimum pilot certification is required to operate an aircraft within Class C airspace?

A student pilot certificate.

[AIM 3-2-4]

19. What minimum equipment is required to operate an aircraft within Class C airspace?

Unless otherwise authorized by the ATC having jurisdiction over the Class C airspace area, no person may operate an aircraft within a Class C airspace area unless that aircraft is equipped with the following:

a. A two-way radio.

b. Automatic pressure altitude reporting equipment having Mode C capability.

[14 CFR 91.130, 91.215]

Chapter 3 **Ground Instruction Requirement**

20. When operating an aircraft through Class C airspace or to an airport within Class C airspace, what basic requirement must be met?

Each person must establish two-way radio communications with the ATC facilities providing air traffic service prior to entering that airspace and thereafter maintain those communications while within that airspace.

[14 CFR 91.130]

21. Two-way radio communications must be established prior to entering Class C airspace. Define the term *established*.

If a controller responds to a radio call with, "(aircraft call sign) standby," radio communications have been established. It is important to understand that if the controller responds to the initial radio call *without* using the aircraft identification, radio communications have *not* been established and the pilot may not enter the Class C airspace.

[AIM 3-2-4]

22. When departing a satellite airport without an operative control tower located within Class C airspace, what requirement must be met?

Each person must establish and maintain two-way radio communications with the ATC facilities having jurisdiction over the Class C airspace area as soon as practicable after departing.

[14 CFR 91.130]

23. What minimum weather conditions are required when conducting VFR flight operations within Class C airspace?

VFR flight operations within Class C airspace require 3 statute miles flight visibility and cloud clearances of at least 500 feet below, 1,000 feet above and 2,000 feet horizontal to clouds.

[14 CFR 91.155]

Chapter 3 **Ground Instruction Requirement**

24. How is Class C airspace depicted on navigational charts?

A solid magenta line is used to depict Class C airspace. Class C airspace is charted on Sectional Charts, IFR En Route Low Altitude, and Terminal Area Charts where appropriate.

[AIM 3-2-4]

25. What type of Air Traffic Control services are provided when operating within Class C airspace?

When two-way communications and radar contact are established within Class C airspace or the Outer Area, participating VFR aircraft will be provided with:

a. Sequencing to the primary airport.
b. Separation from all IFR aircraft.

[AIM 3-2-4]

26. Describe the various types of terminal radar services available for VFR aircraft.

Basic radar service—Safety alerts, traffic advisories, limited radar vectoring (on a workload-permitting basis) and sequencing at locations where procedures have been established for this purpose and/or when covered by a letter of agreement.

TRSA service—Radar sequencing and separation service for VFR aircraft in a TRSA.

Class C service—This service provides, in addition to basic radar service, approved separation between IFR and VFR aircraft, and sequencing of VFR arrivals to the primary airport.

Class B service—Provides, in addition to basic radar service, approved separation of aircraft based on IFR, VFR, and/or weight, and sequencing of VFR arrivals to the primary airport(s).

[AIM 4-1-18]

27. Where are a Mode C transponder and ADS-B Out equipment required?

In general, the regulations require aircraft to be equipped with an operable Mode C transponder and ADS-B Out equipment when operating:

Chapter 3 **Ground Instruction Requirement**

a. In Class A, Class B, or Class C airspace areas;
b. Above the ceiling and within the lateral boundaries of Class B or Class C airspace up to 10,000 feet MSL;
c. In Class E airspace at and above 10,000 feet MSL within the 48 contiguous states and the District of Columbia, excluding the airspace at and below 2,500 feet AGL;
d. Within 30 miles of a Class B airspace primary airport, below 10,000 feet MSL (Mode C Veil);
e. In Class E airspace at and above 3,000 feet MSL over the Gulf of Mexico from the coastline of the United States out to 12 NM;
f. All aircraft flying into, within or across the contiguous United States ADIZ.

Note: Civil and military aircraft should operate with the transponder in the altitude reporting mode and ADS-B Out transmissions enabled (if equipped) at all airports, any time the aircraft is positioned on any portion of an airport movement area. This includes all defined taxiways and runways.

[AIM 4-1-20, 14 CFR 91.215, 91.225, 99.13]

28. What is the ADS-B system?

The Automatic Dependent Surveillance-Broadcast (ADS-B) system is composed of aircraft avionics and a ground infrastructure. Onboard avionics determine the position of the aircraft by using the GNSS and transmit its position along with additional information about the aircraft to ground stations for use by ATC and other ADS-B services. This information is automatically transmitted at a rate of approximately once per second. ADS-B is:

Automatic—because the system automatically broadcasts aircraft position with no external interrogation required.

Dependent—because the system depends on GPS for position information.

Surveillance—because the system provides surveillance information to ATC.

Broadcast—because the system is always broadcasting.

[AIM 4-5-7]

Chapter 3 **Ground Instruction Requirement**

29. What are the two types of ADS-B equipment?

ADS-B Out automatically broadcasts aircraft's GPS position, altitude, velocity, and other information to ATC ground-based surveillance stations as well as directly to other aircraft. ADS-B out is required in all airspace where transponders are required.

ADS-B In is the receipt, processing, and display of ADS-B transmissions. ADS-B In capability is necessary to receive ADS-B traffic and broadcast services (e.g., FIS-B and TIS-B).

[AC 90-114, AIM 4-5-7]

30. What is the maximum speed an aircraft may be operated within Class C airspace?

Unless otherwise authorized or required by ATC, no person may operate an aircraft at or below 2,500 feet above the surface within 4 nautical miles of the primary airport of a Class C or Class D airspace area at an indicated speed of more than 200 knots (230 mph).

[14 CFR 91.117]

31. What is Class D airspace?

Generally, that airspace from the surface to 2,500 feet above the airport elevation (charted in MSL) surrounding those airports that have an operational control tower. The configuration of each Class D airspace area is individually tailored and when instrument procedures are published, the airspace will normally be designed to contain those procedures.

[AIM 3-2-5]

32. When operating an aircraft through Class D airspace or to an airport within Class D airspace, what requirement must be met?

Each person must establish two-way radio communications with the ATC facilities providing air traffic services prior to entering that airspace and thereafter maintain those communications while within that airspace.

[14 CFR 91.129]

Chapter 3 Ground Instruction Requirement

33. When departing a satellite airport without an operative control tower within Class D airspace, what requirement must be met?

Each person must establish and maintain two-way radio communications with the ATC facility having jurisdiction over the Class D airspace area as soon as practicable after departing.

[14 CFR 91.129]

34. Is an ATC clearance required if flight operations are conducted through a Class D arrival extension area?

Arrival extensions for instrument approach procedures may be Class D or Class E airspace. Arrival extensions will either be charted as part of the basic surface area with the blue segmented line indicating Class D airspace or as a separate surface area indicated by the magenta segmented line (Class E airspace). Communications with air traffic control are required whenever you are in the Class D area.

[AIM 3-2-5, 3-2-6]

35. What minimum weather conditions are required when conducting VFR flight operations within Class D airspace?

VFR flight operations within Class D airspace require 3 statute miles flight visibility and cloud clearances of at least 500 feet below, 1,000 feet above and 2,000 feet horizontal to clouds.

[14 CFR 91.155]

36. How is Class D airspace depicted on navigational charts?

Class D airspace areas are depicted on Sectional and Terminal charts with blue segmented lines, and on IFR Low Altitude charts with a boxed [D].

[AIM 3-2-5]

Chapter 3 **Ground Instruction Requirement**

37. What type of air traffic control services are provided when operating within Class D airspace?

No separation services are provided to VFR aircraft. When meteorological conditions permit, regardless of the type of flight plan or whether or not under the control of a radar facility, the pilot is responsible to see and avoid other traffic, terrain, or obstacles. A controller, on a workload permitting basis, will provide radar traffic information, safety alerts and traffic information for sequencing purposes.

[AIM 3-2-5, 5-5-8, 5-5-10]

38. What is the maximum speed an aircraft may be operated within Class D airspace?

Unless otherwise authorized or required by ATC, no person may operate an aircraft at or below 2,500 feet above the surface within 4 nautical miles of the primary airport of a Class C or D airspace area at an indicated airspeed of more than 200 knots (230 mph).

[14 CFR 91.117]

39. What is the definition of Class E airspace?

Generally, if the airspace is not Class A, Class B, Class C, or Class D, and it is controlled airspace, it is Class E airspace.

[AIM 3-2-6]

40. State several examples of Class E airspaoc.

   a. A surface area designated for an airport and configured to contain all instrument approaches.
   b. An extension to a surface area—There are Class E airspace areas that serve as extensions to Class B, Class C, and Class D surface areas designated for an airport. Such airspace provides controlled airspace to contain standard instrument approach procedures.
   c. Airspace used for transition—Class E airspace beginning at either 700 or 1,200 feet AGL used to transition to/from the terminal enroute environment.
   d. En Route Domestic Areas—Class E airspace areas that extend upward from a specified altitude and provide controlled

Chapter 3 Ground Instruction Requirement

airspace in those areas where there is a requirement to provide IFR en route ATC services but the Federal airway system is inadequate.

e. Federal Airways—The Federal airways are Class E airspace areas, and unless otherwise specified, extend upward from 1,200 feet AGL to, but not including 18,000 feet MSL.

f. Offshore Airspace areas—Class E airspace that extends upward from a specified altitude to, but not including 18,000 feet MSL. These areas provide controlled airspace beyond 12 miles from the coast of the United States in those areas where there is a requirement to provide IFR en route ATC services.

g. Unless designated at a lower altitude—Class E airspace begins at 14,500 feet MSL over the United States including that airspace overlying the waters within 12 nautical miles of the coast of the contiguous states and Alaska (excluding the Alaska peninsula west of 160°00'00"W) and the airspace less than 1,500 feet above the surface of the earth.

[AIM 3-2-6]

41. What are the operating rules and pilot/equipment requirements to operate within Class E airspace?

a. Minimum pilot certification—Student Pilot Certificate.

b. No specific equipment requirements in Class E airspace.

c. No specific requirements for arrival or through flight in Class E airspace.

[AIM 3-2-6]

42. What basic operational requirement must be met if flight operations are to be conducted into Class E surface area located at a non-tower airport with a prescribed instrument approach?

As long as the weather allows flight operations to be conducted under basic VFR minimums, a flight into or out of the Class E airspace may be made without an ATC clearance. However, if basic VFR minimums cannot be maintained an ATC clearance will be necessary for arrival or departure (Special VFR clearance).

[AIM 3-2-6]

Chapter 3 **Ground Instruction Requirement**

43. How is Class E airspace depicted on navigational charts?

Class E airspace below 14,500 feet MSL is charted on Sectional, Terminal, World, and IFR En Route Low Altitude charts. Class E airspace without an operating control tower but with prescribed instrument approaches is depicted with a magenta segmented line which denotes controlled airspace extending upward from the surface to the overlying floor of the adjacent controlled airspace. The vertical limit will not be depicted. Where the outer edge of the 700-foot Class E airspace (transition area, magenta shaded line) ends, the 1,200 foot or greater area automatically begins. (Blue shading for Class E airspace beginning at 1,200 feet is used only when it borders Class G airspace.)

[AIM 3-2-6]

44. What is the definition of Class G airspace?

Class G airspace is that portion of the airspace that has not been designated as Class A, B, C, D and E airspace.

[AIM 3-3-1]

45. What is the minimum cloud clearance and visibility required when conducting flight operations in a traffic pattern at night in Class G airspace?

When the visibility is less than 3 statute miles but not less than 1 statute mile during night hours, an airplane may be operated clear of clouds if operated in an airport traffic pattern within one-half mile of the runway.

[14 CFR 91.155]

46. What is the main difference between Class G and Class A, B, C, D, and E airspace?

The main difference that distinguishes Class G (uncontrolled) from Class A, B, C, D, E (controlled) airspace is the flight visibility/cloud clearance requirements necessary to operate within it.

47. What minimum flight visibility and clearance from clouds are required for VFR flight in the following situations?

CLASS C, D, or E AIRSPACE (controlled airspace)
Less than 10,000 feet MSL:
Visibility: 3 statute miles.
Cloud clearance: 500 feet below, 1,000 feet above, 2,000 feet horizontal.

At or above 10,000 feet MSL:
Visibility: 5 statute miles.
Cloud clearance: 1,000 feet below, 1,000 feet above, 1 statute mile horizontal.

CLASS G AIRSPACE (uncontrolled airspace)
1,200 feet or less above the surface (regardless of MSL altitude):
DAY: Visibility: 1 statute mile.
Cloud clearance: clear of clouds.
NIGHT: Visibility: 3 statute miles.
Cloud clearance: 500 feet below, 1,000 feet above, 2,000 feet horizontal.

*More than 1,200 feet above the surface but **less than** 10,000 feet MSL:*
DAY: Visibility: 1 statute mile.
Cloud clearance: 500 feet below, 1,000 feet above, 2,000 feet horizontal.
NIGHT: Visibility: 3 statute miles.
Cloud clearance: 500 feet below, 1,000 feet above, 2,000 feet horizontal.

*More than 1,200 feet above the surface and **at or above** 10,000 feet MSL:*
Visibility: 5 statute miles.
Cloud clearance: 1,000 feet below, 1,000 feet above, 1 statute mile horizontal.

[14 CFR 91.155]

Chapter 3 Ground Instruction Requirement

48. If VFR flight minimums cannot be maintained, can a VFR flight be made into Class B, C, D, or E airspace?

No, with one exception. A special VFR clearance may be obtained from the controlling authority prior to entering the Class B, C, D, or E airspace provided the flight can be made clear of clouds with at least one statute mile ground visibility if taking off or landing. If ground visibility is not reported at that airport, the flight visibility must be at least 1 statute mile.

[AIM 4-4-6]

49. Are special VFR clearances always available to pilots in all classes of airspace?

A VFR pilot may request and be given a clearance to enter, leave, or operate within most Class D and Class E surface areas and some Class B and Class C surface areas, traffic permitting, and providing such flight will not delay IFR operations.

Note: Special VFR operations by fixed-wing aircraft are prohibited in some Class B and Class C surface areas due to the volume of IFR traffic; a list of these areas is contained in 14 CFR Part 91 and also depicted on sectional aeronautical charts.

[AIM 4-4-6]

50. If it becomes apparent that a special VFR clearance will be necessary, what facility should the pilot contact in order to obtain one?

Within the Class B, C, or D surface area, requests for clearances should be to the tower. If no tower is located within the airspace (Class E airspace), a clearance may be obtained from the nearest tower, flight service, or center.

[AIM 4-4-6]

51. Can a special VFR clearance be obtained into or out of Class B, C, D, or E airspace at night?

Special VFR operations by fixed-wing aircraft are prohibited between sunset and sunrise unless the pilot is instrument rated and the aircraft is equipped for IFR flight.

[AIM 4-4-6]

Chapter 3 Ground Instruction Requirement

52. Under what conditions, if any, may pilots enter restricted or prohibited areas?

No person may operate an aircraft within a restricted area contrary to the restrictions imposed, or within a prohibited area, unless that person has the permission of the using or controlling agency.

Normally, *no* operations are permitted within a prohibited area and *prior* permission must always be obtained before operating within a restricted area.

[14 CFR 91.133]

53. What is a TRSA?

A terminal radar service area (TRSA) consists of airspace surrounding designated airports wherein ATC provides radar vectoring, sequencing, and separation on a full-time basis for all IFR and participating VFR aircraft. Pilot participation is urged but not mandatory.

[AIM 3-5-6]

54. What class of airspace is a TRSA?

TRSAs do not fit into any of the U.S. airspace classes and are not contained in 14 CFR Part 71 nor are there any operating rules in Part 91. The primary airport(s) within the TRSA become Class D airspace. The remaining portion of a TRSA overlies other controlled airspace which is normally Class E airspace beginning at 700 or 1,200 feet and established to transition to/from the en route/terminal environment. TRSAs will continue to be an airspace area where participating pilots can receive additional radar services which have been redefined as TRSA service.

[AIM 3-5-6]

55. How are TRSAs depicted on navigational charts?

TRSAs are depicted on visual charts with a solid black line and altitudes for each segment. The Class D portion is charted with a blue segmented line.

[AIM 3-5-6]

Chapter 3 Ground Instruction Requirement

56. What are TFRs?

A Temporary Flight Restriction (TFR) is a type of Notice to Air Missions (NOTAM). A TFR defines an area restricted to air travel due to a hazardous condition, a special event, or a general warning for the entire FAA airspace.

While not all inclusive, a TFR may be issued for the following reasons: toxic gas leaks or spills, fumes from flammable agents which, if fanned by rotor or propeller wash, could endanger persons or property on the surface or in other aircraft; volcanic eruptions that could endanger airborne aircraft and occupants; hijacking incidents that may endanger persons or property on the surface, or airborne aircraft and occupants; aircraft accident/incident sites; aviation or ground resources engaged in wildfire suppression; aircraft relief activities following a disaster; aerial demonstrations or major sporting events.

[FAA-H-8083-25]

57. How do you know if a TFR affects your planned flight?

TFRs are not depicted on charts. Pilots are notified of them through the NOTAM process. TFR NOTAMs must comply with procedures detailed in FAA Order 7930.2, Notices to Air Missions (NOTAM). Many modern EFB flight planning software options include these TFR depictions additionally.

[FAA-H-8083-25]

58. How may a pilot get information about TFRs timing and location?

National Airspace System (NAS) users or other interested parties should contact the nearest flight service station, or (in CONUS) the appropriate ARTCC for TFR information. Additionally, you can find TFR information on automated briefings and at any of the following sources:

TFR List: tfr.faa.gov/tfr2/list.html

TFR Graphical: tfr.faa.gov/tfr_map_ims/html/index.html

Domestic Notices: www.faa.gov/air_traffic/publications/domesticnotices/

International Notices: www.faa.gov/air_traffic/publications/internationalnotices/

FAA NOTAM Search: notams.aim.faa.gov/notamSearch/
FCFSS website: 1800wxbrief.com/
[FAA Order 7210.3DD]

R. National Transportation Safety Board

1. When is immediate notification to the NTSB required?

The operator of any civil aircraft, or any public aircraft not operated by the Armed Forces or an intelligence agency of the United States, or any foreign aircraft shall immediately, and by the most expeditious means available, notify the nearest National Transportation Safety Board (NTSB) office, when:

An aircraft accident or any of the following listed serious incidents occur:

(1) Flight control system malfunction or failure;

(2) Inability of any required flight crewmember to perform normal flight duties as a result of injury or illness;

(3) Failure of any internal turbine engine component that results in the escape of debris other than out the exhaust path;

(4) In-flight fire;

(5) Aircraft collision in flight;

(6) Damage to property, other than the aircraft, estimated to exceed $25,000 for repair (including materials and labor) or fair market value in the event of total loss, whichever is less.

(7) For large multiengine aircraft (more than 12,500 pounds maximum certificated takeoff weight):

(i) In-flight failure of electrical systems which requires the sustained use of an emergency bus powered by a back-up source such as a battery, auxiliary power unit, or air-driven generator to retain flight control or essential instruments;

(ii) In-flight failure of hydraulic systems that results in sustained reliance on the sole remaining hydraulic or mechanical system for movement of flight control surfaces;

(iii) Sustained loss of the power or thrust produced by two or more engines; and

(iv) An evacuation of an aircraft in which an emergency egress system is utilized.

(8) Release of all or a portion of a propeller blade from an aircraft, excluding release caused solely by ground contact;

(9) A complete loss of information, excluding flickering, from more than 50 percent of an aircraft's cockpit displays known as:

    (i) Electronic Flight Instrument System (EFIS) displays;

    (ii) Engine Indication and Crew Alerting System (EICAS) displays;

    (iii) Electronic Centralized Aircraft Monitor (ECAM) displays; or

    (iv) Other displays of this type, which generally include a primary flight display (PFD), primary navigation display (PND), and other integrated displays;

(10) Airborne Collision and Avoidance System (ACAS) resolution advisories issued when an aircraft is being operated on an instrument flight rules flight plan and compliance with the advisory is necessary to avert a substantial risk of collision between two or more aircraft.

(11) Damage to helicopter tail or main rotor blades, including ground damage, that requires major repair or replacement of the blade(s);

(12) Any event in which an operator, when operating an airplane as an air carrier at a public-use airport on land:

    (i) Lands or departs on a taxiway, incorrect runway, or other area not designed as a runway; or

    (ii) Experiences a runway incursion that requires the operator or the crew of another aircraft or vehicle to take immediate corrective action to avoid a collision.

(13) An aircraft is overdue and is believed to have been involved in an accident.

[NTSB 830]

Chapter 3 **Ground Instruction Requirement**

S. Airport Operations

1. What is the standard direction of turns when approaching an uncontrolled airport for landing?

Each pilot of an airplane must make all turns of that airplane to the left unless the airport displays approved light signals or visual markings indicating that turns should be made to the right, in which case the pilot must make all turns to the right.

[14 CFR 91.126, AC90-66, FAA-H-8083-3, AIM 4-3-4]

2. What is considered standard for traffic pattern altitude?

Unless otherwise established, 1,000 feet AGL is the recommended traffic pattern altitude. At most airports and military air bases, traffic pattern altitudes for propeller-driven aircraft generally extend from 600 feet to as high as 1,500 feet AGL. Also, traffic pattern altitudes for military turbojet aircraft sometimes extend up to 2,500 feet AGL. A pilot should check FAA Chart Supplement data for the airport to be used to determine if a different traffic pattern altitude has been established.

[AIM 4-3-3]

3. When issued taxi instructions at an airport with a control tower in operation, if the controller issues a taxi clearance that takes you to the takeoff runway, are you automatically authorized to cross any intermediate runway that intersects your taxi route?

No; Aircraft must receive a runway crossing clearance for each runway that their taxi route crosses. When assigned a takeoff runway, ATC will first specify the runway, issue taxi instructions, and state any hold short instructions or runway crossing clearances if the taxi route will cross a runway. When issuing taxi instructions to any point other than an assigned takeoff runway, ATC will specify the point to taxi to, issue taxi instructions, and state any hold short instructions or runway crossing clearances if the taxi route will cross a runway. ATC is required to obtain a readback from the pilot of all runway hold short instructions.

[AIM 4-3-18]

Chapter 3 **Ground Instruction Requirement**

4. Where are wake turbulence and wing-tip vortices likely to occur?

All aircraft generate turbulence and associated wing-tip vortices. In general, avoid the area behind and below the generating aircraft, especially at low altitudes. Also of concern is the weight, speed, and shape of the wing of the generating aircraft. The greatest vortex strength occurs when the generating aircraft is HEAVY, CLEAN, and SLOW.

[AIM 7-3-3]

5. What operational procedures should be followed when wake vortices are suspected to exist?

a. *Landing behind large aircraft on the same runway:* stay at or above the large aircraft's flight path. Note its touchdown point and land beyond it.

b. *Landing behind a departing large aircraft:* note the large aircraft's rotation point; land well prior to its rotation point.

c. *Departing behind a large aircraft on the same runway:* note the large aircraft's rotation point and rotate prior to its rotation point. Continue to climb above and upwind of its flight path.

d. *En route VFR:* avoid flight below and behind a large aircraft's path.

[AIM 7-3-6]

6. What is LAHSO?

An acronym for land and hold short operations. These include landing and holding short of an intersecting runway, an intersecting taxiway, or some other designated point on a runway. LAHSO is an ATC procedure that requires pilot participation to balance the needs for increased airport capacity and system efficiency.

[AIM 4-3-11]

7. Is a pilot required to comply with or accept a LAHSO clearance?

A pilot is not required to accept a LAHSO clearance. Student pilots or pilots not familiar with LAHSO should not participate in the program. Pilots are expected to decline a LAHSO clearance if they determine it will compromise safety or if weather is below basic

VFR weather conditions (a minimum ceiling of 1,000 feet and 3 SM visibility). If a LAHSO clearance is accepted the pilot must comply with that clearance.

[AIM 4-3-11]

8. Where can available landing distance (ALD) data be found?

ALD data is published in the special notices section of the *Chart Supplement*. and in the U.S. Terminal Procedures Publications. Controllers will also provide ALD data upon request.

[AIM 4-3-11]

9. What are the six types of signs installed at airports?

a. *Mandatory instruction sign*—red background/white inscription; denotes an entrance to a runway, a critical area, or a prohibited area.

b. *Location sign*—black background/yellow inscription/yellow border; do not have arrows; used to identify a taxiway or runway location, the boundary of the runway, or identify an ILS critical area.

c. *Direction sign*—yellow background/black identifies the designation of the intersecting taxiway(s) leading out of an intersection that a pilot would expect to turn onto or hold short of.

d. *Destination sign*—yellow background/black inscription and also contain arrows; provides information on locating runways, terminals, cargo areas, and civil aviation areas, etc.

e. *Information sign*—yellow background/black inscription; used to provide the pilot with information on areas that can't be seen from the control tower, applicable radio frequencies, and noise abatement procedures, etc.

f. *Runway distance remaining sign*—black background/white numeral inscription; indicates the distance of the remaining runway in thousands of feet.

[AIM 2-3-9 through 2-3-13]

Chapter 3 Ground Instruction Requirement

10. What color are runway markings? Taxiway markings?

Markings for runways are white. Markings for taxiways, areas not intended for use by aircraft (closed and hazardous areas), and holding positions (even if they are on a runway) are yellow.

[AIM 2-3-2]

11. What airport marking aids will be used to indicate the following?

Runway threshold markings — These come in two configurations. They either consist of eight longitudinal stripes of uniform dimensions disposed symmetrically about the runway centerline, or the number of stripes is related to the runway width. A threshold marking helps identify the beginning of the runway available for landing.

Displaced threshold — A threshold located at a point on the runway other than the designated beginning of the runway. A displaced threshold reduces the length of runway available for landings. The portion of runway behind a displaced threshold is available for takeoffs in either direction. A ten-foot wide white threshold bar is located across the width of the runway at the displaced threshold. White arrows are located along the centerline in the area between the beginning of the runway and displaced threshold. White arrowheads are located across the width of the runway just prior to the threshold bar.

Runway hold position markings — For taxiways, these markings indicate where an aircraft is supposed to stop when it does not have clearance to proceed onto the runway. They are also installed on runways only if the runway is normally used by air traffic control for land and hold short operations. They consist of four yellow lines, two solid and two dashed, spaced six inches apart and extending across the width of the taxiway or runway.

Temporarily closed runways and taxiways — Provides a visual indication to pilots that a runway/taxiway is temporarily closed. Yellow crosses are placed on the runway only at each end of the runway. Closed taxiways are blocked with barricades or may utilize a yellow cross at the entrance to the taxiway.

Permanently closed runways and taxiways — For runways and taxiways which are permanently closed, the lighting circuits will be disconnected. The runway threshold, runway designation, and touchdown markings are obliterated and yellow crosses are placed at each end of the runway and at 1,000-foot intervals.

[AIM 2-3-2 through 2-3-6]

12. When is V_Y used on climbout?

Upon liftoff, the airplane should be flying at approximately the pitch attitude that allows it to accelerate to V_Y. This is the speed at which the airplane gains the most altitude in the shortest period of time.

[FAA-H-8083-3]

13. When is V_X used on climbout?

When performing takeoffs and climbs from fields where the takeoff area is short or the available takeoff area is restricted by obstructions, the pilot should operate the airplane at the maximum limit of its takeoff performance capabilities. V_X is the speed at which the airplane achieves the greatest gain in altitude for a given distance over the ground. It is usually slightly less than V_Y, which is the greatest gain in altitude per unit of time.

[FAA-H-8083-3]

14. What is a stabilized approach?

A stabilized approach is one in which the pilot establishes and maintains a constant angle glide path towards a predetermined point on the landing runway. It is based on the pilot's judgment of certain visual clues and depends on the maintenance of a constant final descent airspeed and configuration.

[FAA-H-8083-3]

Chapter 3 **Ground Instruction Requirement**

15. What should the pilot do if unable to maintain a stabilized approach?

Approaches which are not stabilized can lead to a LOC accident. A stabilized approach is one in which the pilot establishes and maintains a constant angle glide path towards a predetermined point on the landing runway; it means the glidepath is set (the airplane is on the correct flightpath), the airplane is tracking the extended centerline of the runway, the descent rate is constant and generally no greater than 500 feet per minute, power setting is appropriate for the approach configuration, and all but the final landing checklist are complete. If a pilot is unable to maintain a stabilized approach they should initiate a go-around.

[FAA-H-8083-3]

T. Runway Incursion Avoidance

1. What are three major areas that contribute to runway incursions?

a. *Communications*—misunderstanding the given clearance; failure to communicate effectively

b. *Airport knowledge*—failure to navigate the airport correctly; unable to interpret airport signage

c. *Cockpit procedures for maintaining orientation*—failure to maintain situational awareness

[FAA-H-8083-3]

2. Preflight planning for taxi operations should be an integral part of the pilot's flight planning process. What information should this include?

a. Review and understand airport signage, markings and lighting.

b. Review the airport diagram, planned taxi route, and identify any hot spots.

c. Review the latest airfield NOTAMs and ATIS (if available) for taxiway/runway closures, construction activity, etc.

d. Conduct a pre-taxi/pre-landing briefing that includes the expected/assigned taxi route and any hold short lines and restrictions based on ATIS information or previous experience at the airport.

e. Plan for critical times and locations on the taxi route (complex intersections, crossing runways, etc.).

f. Plan to complete as many aircraft checklist items as possible prior to taxi.

[AC 91-73]

3. What is an airport hot spot?

A hot spot is a runway safety-related problem area or intersection on an airport. Typically, hot spots are complex or confusing taxiway–taxiway or taxiway–runway intersections. A lack of visibility may exist at certain points and/or the tower may be unable to see those particular intersections. Pilots should be increasingly vigilant when approaching and taxiing through these intersections. Pilots can find these on airport diagrams in FAA Chart Supplement documents.

[FAA-H-8083-16]

4. Why is use of sterile cockpit procedures important when conducting taxi operations?

Pilots must be able to focus on their duties without being distracted by non-flight-related matters unrelated to the safe and proper operation of the aircraft. Refraining from nonessential activities during ground operations is essential. Passengers should be briefed on the importance of minimizing conversations and questions during taxi as well as on arrival, from the time landing preparations begin until the aircraft is safely parked.

[AC 91-73]

5. When should a pilot request progressive taxi instructions?

If the pilot is unfamiliar with the airport or for any reason confusion exists as to the correct taxi routing, a request may be made for progressive taxi instructions, which include step-by-step routing directions.

[AIM 4-3-18]

Chapter 3 **Ground Instruction Requirement**

6. **After completing your pre-taxi/pre-landing briefing of the taxi route you expect to receive, ATC calls and gives you a different route. What potential pitfall is common in this situation?**

   A common pitfall of pre-taxi and pre-landing planning is setting expectations and then receiving different instructions from ATC. Pilots need to follow the instructions that they actually receive, and not the ones they expect to receive. Short term memory is of limited duration. The best antidote is to write down the new clearance information.

   [AC 91-73]

7. **Why is it a good idea to write down taxi instructions, especially at larger or unfamiliar airports?**

   Writing down taxi instructions, especially complex instructions, can reduce a pilot's vulnerability to forgetting part of the instructions and provides a reference for read-back of instructions to ATC. It can also be used as a means of reconfirming the taxi route and any restrictions at any time during taxi operations.

   [AC 91-73]

8. **When issued taxi instructions to an assigned takeoff runway, are you automatically authorized to cross any runway that intersects your taxi route?**

   No; aircraft must receive a runway crossing clearance for each runway that their taxi route crosses. When assigned a takeoff runway, ATC will first specify the runway, issue taxi instructions, and state any hold short instructions or runway crossing clearances if the taxi route will cross a runway. When issuing taxi instructions to any point other than an assigned takeoff runway, ATC will specify the point to which to taxi, issue taxi instructions, and state any hold short instructions or runway crossing clearances if the taxi route will cross a runway. ATC is required to obtain a read back from the pilot of all runway hold short instructions.

   [AIM 4-3-18]

Chapter 3 Ground Instruction Requirement

9. **When receiving taxi instructions from a controller, pilots should always read back what information?**
   a. The runway assignment.
   b. Any clearance to enter a specific runway.
   c. Any instruction to hold short of a specific runway or line up and wait.

   [AIM 4-3-18]

10. **While taxiing at a towered airport, should a pilot leave their transponder on or set it to Standby?**

    The FAA encourages pilots to leave their transponder in an active mode during all movement operations. During taxi to parking or when leaving a parking spot to taxi to active runways for departure the transponder should be activated. The standby mode should only be engaged if the controller requests it or if the aircraft is in a parking space and will not be moving.

    [AC90-114]

11. **What are some recommended practices that can assist a pilot in maintaining situational awareness during taxi operations?**
    a. A current airport diagram should be available for immediate reference during taxi.
    b. Monitor ATC instructions/clearances issued to other aircraft for the big picture.
    c. Focus attention outside the cockpit while taxiing.
    d. Use all available resources (airport diagrams, airport signs, markings, lighting, and ATC) to keep the aircraft on its assigned taxi route.
    e. Cross-reference heading indicator to ensure turns are being made in the correct direction and that you're on the assigned taxi route.
    f. Prior to crossing any hold short line, visually check for conflicting traffic; verbalize, "clear left, clear right."
    g. Be alert for other aircraft with similar call signs on the frequency.

    (continued)

Chapter 3 **Ground Instruction Requirement**

    h. Understand and follow all ATC instructions and if in doubt—Ask!

    i. Use an EFB device that shows the aircraft position overlaid on an airport diagram.

    j. Use in panel aircraft charting and aircraft position depictions on an airport diagram if available.

[AC 91-73]

12. How can a pilot use aircraft exterior lighting to enhance situational awareness and safety during airport surface operations?

To the extent possible and consistent with aircraft equipment, operating limitations, and pilot procedures, pilots should illuminate exterior lights as follows:

    a. *Engines running*—Turn on the rotating beacon whenever an engine is running.

    b. *Taxiing*—Prior to commencing taxi, turn on navigation/position lights and anti-collision lights.

    c. *Crossing a runway*—All exterior lights should be illuminated when crossing a runway.

    d. *Entering the departure runway for takeoff*—All exterior lights (except landing lights) should be on to make your aircraft more conspicuous to aircraft on final and ATC.

    e. *Cleared for takeoff*—All exterior lights including takeoff/landing lights.

Note: If you see an aircraft in takeoff position on a runway with landing lights ON, that aircraft has most likely received its takeoff clearance and will be departing immediately.

[AC 91-73, SAFO]

13. During calm or nearly calm wind conditions, at an airport without an operating control tower, a pilot should be aware of what potentially hazardous situations?

Aircraft may be landing and/or taking off on more than one runway at the airport. Also, aircraft may be using an instrument approach procedure to runways other than the runway in use for

Chapter 3 **Ground Instruction Requirement**

VFR operations. The instrument approach runway may intersect the VFR runway. It is also possible that an instrument arrival may be made to the opposite end of the runway from which a takeoff is being made.

[AC 91-73]

14. You have just landed at a tower-controlled airport and missed your assigned taxiway for exiting the runway. Is it permissible for you to turn around on the runway and return to the exit taxiway?

No; at airports with an operating control tower, pilots should never stop or reverse course on the runway without first obtaining ATC approval.

[AIM 4-3-20]

15. When taxiing at a non-towered airport, what are several precautionary measures you should take prior to entering or crossing a runway?

Listen on the appropriate frequency (CTAF) for inbound aircraft information and always scan the full length of the runway, including the final approach and departure paths, before entering or crossing the runway. Self-announce your position and intentions and remember that not all aircraft are radio-equipped.

[AC 91-73]

16. ATC has instructed you to line up and wait on the departure runway due to crossing traffic on an intersecting taxiway. What is considered a reasonable amount of time to wait for a takeoff clearance before calling ATC?

FAA analysis of accidents and incidents involving aircraft holding in position indicate that two minutes or more elapsed between the time the instruction was issued to line up and wait and the resulting event (for example, land-over or go-around). If you have been holding in position on the runway for more than 90 seconds, or you see or hear a potential conflict, contact ATC immediately.

[AIM 5-2-4, SAFO]

17. What is a pilot deviation?

A pilot deviation (PD) is defined as an action of a pilot that results in the violation of a Federal aviation regulation. PDs are broadly classified as either airborne deviations or surface deviations. Within each of these two broad classifications are a number of sub-classifications. The principal areas of concern in the airborne classification include altitude deviations, course deviations, and airspace incursions. The principal area of concern within the surface deviation classification involves runway incursions, but surface deviations also include vehicle/pedestrian violations. While the outcomes of most PDs are benign, any deviation has the potential to be catastrophic. Because of this potential for catastrophic outcome, PDs are a major concern in both the aviation industry and within the FAA. For several years, PDs have been on the rise. Of particular concern is that a significant majority of all PDs (69%) are occurring during GA operations. The occurrence of incidents and PDs has emphasized the need to ensure that all pilots receive adequate briefing on PD avoidance awareness. Pilots should be familiar with all types of airspace, and ground operating procedures, and best practices to avoid potential PDs. The flight review may be the only regular proficiency and recurrency training experienced by some pilots. Therefore, CFIs should place appropriate emphasis on this part of the review.

[AC 61-98]

U. Aviation Security

1. What are several actions you can take to enhance aircraft security?

a. Always lock your aircraft.

b. Keep track of door/ignition keys and don't leave keys in unattended aircraft.

c. Use secondary locks (prop, tie down, throttle, and wheel locks) or aircraft disabler if available.

d. Lock hangar when unattended.

[TSA]

Chapter 3 Ground Instruction Requirement

2. What type of airport security procedures should you review regularly to prevent unauthorized access to aircraft at your airport?

   a. Limitations on ramp access to people other than instructors and students.
   b. Standards for securing aircraft on the ramp.
   c. Securing access to aircraft keys at all times.
   d. New auxiliary security items for aircraft (prop locks, throttle locks, locking tie downs).
   e. After-hours or weekend access procedures.

   [TSA]

3. What might be some examples of what you would consider suspicious activity at an airport?

   a. Aircraft with unusual modifications (such as modified N-numbers) or activity.
   b. Unfamiliar persons loitering for extended periods in the vicinity of parked aircraft.
   c. Anyone making threats.
   d. Events or circumstances that do not fit the pattern of lawful, normal activity at an airport.
   e. Pilots appearing to be under the control of others.

   [TSA]

4. When witnessing suspicious or criminal activity, what are three basic ways for reporting the suspected activity?

   If you determine that it's safe, question the individual. If their response is unsatisfactory and they continue to act suspiciously:

   a. Alert airport or FBO management.
   b. Contact local law enforcement if the activity poses an immediate threat to persons or property.
   c. Contact the 866-GA-SECURE hotline to document the reported event.

   [TSA]

Chapter 3 **Ground Instruction Requirement**

5. **What is the purpose of the 866-GA-SECURE phone number?**

   866-GA-SECURE is a toll-free hotline operated by the Transportation Security Administration (TSA) Security Operations Center. It is staffed 24/7 to take reports of suspicious or criminal activity occurring at general aviation airports. TSA personnel will document the reported activity, collect your personal contact numbers, and pass the information on to the appropriate regulatory office within the TSA.

   Note: Calling 866-GA-SECURE will not dispatch local law enforcement. In the event of an immediate emergency, 911 or local law enforcement should be contacted first.

   [TSA]

6. **What are several sources of information available to pilots interested in additional guidance on aviation security?**

   Security Guidelines for General Aviation Airports is a set of federally endorsed guidelines that offers an extensive list of options, ideas, and suggestions for the airport operator, sponsor, tenant and/or user to choose from when considering security enhancements for GA facilities.

   Flight School Security Awareness Training for Aircraft and Simulators is an online training course designed to raise the general security awareness levels of employees working in the flight training industry.

   [TSA]

V. Aircraft and Engine Operations

1. **How many magnetos does your aircraft have and what do they do for the engine?**

   Most general aviation aircraft have two magnetos per engine for redundancy and safety. This dual ignition system ensures that the engine can still operate if one magneto fails. Pilots can typically switch between using both magnetos and relying on a single magneto during normal operation or in the event of a magneto malfunction.

   [FAA-H-8083-25]

Chapter 3 **Ground Instruction Requirement**

2. **What type of fuel does your aircraft require (minimum octane rating and color)?**

   Most general aviation aircraft operate on 100LL fuel and the color is blue. A few light general aviation aircraft do operate on diesel fuel (Jet A) which would be a straw like color. Some additional fuels are available such as UL91, UL94 or G100L. Older aircraft may have been designed to operate on 80 octane avgas and be able to operate on auto gasoline that does not contain ethanol and is of a higher octane with STC approval. Turbine aircraft will typically operate on Jet A fuel. Know what fuel your aircraft can use and how to identify it when filling the aircraft fuel tanks to ensure proper fueling has taken place.

3. **Can other types of fuel be used if the specified grade is not available?**

   A pilot can typically use a higher grade of fuel than what an engine is originally certificated to use. A lower grade should never be used. If you must use a different grade of fuel, use a grade as close as possible to 100LL Always reference the aircraft's AFM or POH or supplemental type certificate approvals to determine what fuels can be used in an aircraft with the engine.

   [FAA-H-8083-25]

4. **Is your aircraft engine fuel injected or carbureted?**

   Knowing if your aircraft has a carburetor system or is fuel injected can help a pilot identify potential in flight problems and better manage power settings and fuel flows during flight. A fuel injected aircraft will not be susceptible to carburetor icing but may in some situations, especially during high ambient temperatures, fuel injection systems may be susceptible to vapor lock. Vapor lock occurs when the fuel in the lines vaporizes before reaching the engine, causing a disruption in fuel delivery.

   [FAA-H-8083-25]

Chapter 3 **Ground Instruction Requirement**

W. System and Equipment Malfunctions

1. What causes carburetor icing and what are the first indications of its presence?

The vaporization of fuel, combined with the expansion of air as it passes through the carburetor, causes a sudden cooling of the mixture. The temperature of the air passing through the carburetor may drop as much as 60°F within a fraction of a second. Water vapor is squeezed out by this cooling, and if the temperature in the carburetor reaches 32°F or below, the moisture will be deposited as frost or ice inside the carburetor. For airplanes with a fixed-pitch propeller, the first indication of carburetor icing is loss of rpm. For airplanes with controllable-pitch (constant-speed) propellers, the first indication is usually a drop in manifold pressure.

[FAA-H-8083-25]

2. What action should be taken if detonation is suspected?

Corrective action for detonation may be accomplished by adjusting any of the engine controls which will reduce both temperature and pressure of the fuel air charge.

a. Reduce power.
b. Reduce the climb rate for better cooling.
c. Enrich the fuel/air mixture.
d. Open cowl flaps if available.

Also, ensure that the airplane has been serviced with the proper grade of fuel.

[FAA-H-8083-25]

3. Under what kind of conditions should a pilot consider carburetor icing to be most probable?

The reduced air pressure, as well as the vaporization of fuel, contributes to the temperature decrease in the carburetor. Ice generally forms in the vicinity of the throttle valve and in the venturi throat. This restricts the flow of the fuel-air mixture and reduces power. If enough ice builds up, the engine may cease to operate. Carburetor ice is most likely to occur when temperatures are below 70°F or 21°C and the relative humidity is above 80 percent. Due to the sudden cooling that takes place in the carburetor, icing can occur even in outside air temperatures as high as 100°F (38°C) and humidity as low as 50 percent. This temperature drop can be as much as 60 to 70 absolute (versus relative) Fahrenheit degrees ($70 \times 100/180 = 38.89$ Celsius degrees) (Remember there are 180 Fahrenheit degrees from freezing to boiling versus 100 degrees for the Celsius scale.) Therefore, an outside air temperature of 100°F (38°C), a temperature drop of an absolute 70°F (38.89°C) results in an air temperature in the carburetor of 30°F (−1°C).

[FAA-H-8083-25]

4. How would a pilot know if their engine is experiencing preignition?

One of the most common signs of preignition is a pinging or knocking sound coming from the engine. This noise is often described as a metallic rattling or knocking and is caused by the rapid, uncontrolled burning of the fuel-air mixture.

- Preignition can result in a loss of engine power because the combustion process is not occurring in a controlled manner. Premature ignition can cause a reduction in the engine's efficiency and overall performance.

- Preignition can contribute to increased engine temperatures. The rapid combustion generates more heat than the engine can effectively dissipate, leading to higher operating temperatures.

- Preignition may cause the engine to backfire, where combustion occurs in the intake manifold or exhaust system rather than within the combustion chamber.

- In severe cases, preignition can cause the engine to stall or hesitate. This is especially true if the preignition disrupts the normal combustion process to the point where the engine cannot continue running smoothly.

[FAA-H-8083-25]

5. What actions should be taken if preignition is suspected?

Corrective actions for preignition include any type of engine operation which would promote cooling such as:

a. Enrich the fuel/air mixture.
b. Reduce power.
c. Reduce the climb rate for better cooling.
d. Open cowl flaps if available.

[FAA-H-8083-25]

6. Interpret the following ammeter indications.

Ammeter indicates a right deflection (positive).

- *After starting*—Power from the battery used for starting is being replenished by the alternator; or, if a full-scale charge is indicated for more than 1 minute, the starter is still engaged and a shutdown is indicated.
- *During flight*—A faulty voltage regulator is causing the alternator to overcharge the battery. Reset the system and if the condition continues, terminate the flight as soon as possible.

Ammeter indicates a left deflection (negative).

- *After starting*—It is normal during start. At other times this indicates the alternator is not functioning or an overload condition exists in the system. The battery is not receiving a charge.
- *During flight*—The alternator is not functioning or an overload exists in the system. The battery is not receiving a charge. Possible causes: the master switch was accidentally shut off, or the alternator circuit breaker tripped.

Chapter 3 Ground Instruction Requirement

7. **What action should be taken if the ammeter indicates a continuous discharge while in flight?**

   The alternator has quit producing a charge, so the alternator circuit breaker should be checked and reset if necessary. If this does not correct the problem, the following should be accomplished:

   a. The alternator should be turned off; pull the circuit breaker (the field circuit will continue to draw power from the battery).

   b. All electrical equipment not essential to flight should be turned off (the battery is now the only source of electrical power).

8. **What action should be taken if the ammeter indicates a continuous charge while in flight (more than two needle widths)?**

   If a continuous excessive rate of charge were allowed for any extended period of time, the battery would overheat and evaporate the electrolyte at an excessive rate. A possible explosion of the battery could result. Also, electronic components in the electrical system would be adversely affected by higher than normal voltage. Protection is provided by an overvoltage sensor which will shut the alternator down if an excessive voltage is detected. If this should occur, the following should be done:

   a. The alternator should be turned off; pull the circuit breaker (the field circuit will continue to draw power from the battery).

   b. All electrical equipment not essential to flight should be turned off (the battery is now the only source of electrical power).

   c. The flight should be terminated and a landing made as soon as possible.

9. **During a cross-country flight you notice that the oil pressure is low, but the oil temperature is normal. What is the problem and what action should be taken?**

   A low oil pressure in flight could be the result of any one of several problems, the most common being that of insufficient oil. If the oil temperature continues to remain normal, a clogged oil pressure relief valve or an oil pressure gauge malfunction could be the culprit. In any case, a landing at the nearest airport is advisable to check for the cause of trouble.

Chapter 3 Ground Instruction Requirement

10. What procedures should be followed concerning a partial loss of power in flight?

If a partial loss of power occurs, the first priority is to establish and maintain a suitable airspeed (best glide airspeed if necessary). Then, select an emergency landing area and remain within gliding distance. As time allows, attempt to determine the cause and correct it. Complete the following checklist:

a. Check the carburetor heat.

b. Check the amount of fuel in each tank and switch fuel tanks if necessary.

c. Check the fuel selector valve's current position.

d. Check the mixture control.

e. Check that the primer control is all the way in and locked.

f. Check the operation of the magnetos in all three positions; both, left or right.

11. What procedures should be followed if an engine fire develops on the ground during starting?

Continue to attempt an engine start as a start will cause flames and excess fuel to be sucked back through the carburetor.

a. If the engine starts:
- Increase the power to a higher RPM for a few moments; and
- shut down the engine and inspect it.

b. If the engine does not start:
- Set the throttle to the "Full" position.
- Set the mixture control to "Idle cutoff."
- Continue to try an engine start in an attempt to put out the fire by vacuum.

c. If the fire continues:
- Turn the ignition switch to "Off."
- Turn the master switch to "Off."
- Set the fuel selector to "Off."

In all cases, evacuate the aircraft and obtain a fire extinguisher and/or fire personnel assistance.

12. What procedures should be followed if an engine fire develops in flight?

In the event of an engine fire in flight, the following procedures should be used:

a. Set the mixture control to "Idle cutoff."
b. Set the fuel selector valve to "Off."
c. Turn the master switch to "Off."
d. Set the cabin heat and air vents to "Off"; leave the overhead vents "On."
e. Establish an airspeed of 100 KIAS and increase the descent, if necessary, to find an airspeed that will provide for an incombustible mixture.
f. Execute a forced landing procedures checklist.

X. Airplane Instruments/Systems

1. What compass errors may a pilot need to compensate for during flight operations?

Oscillation error—Erratic movement of the compass card caused by turbulence or rough control technique.

Deviation error—Due to electrical and magnetic disturbances in the aircraft.

Variation error—Angular difference between true and magnetic north; reference isogonic lines of variation.

Dip errors:

  Acceleration error—On east or west headings, while accelerating, the magnetic compass shows a turn to the north, and when decelerating, it shows a turn to the south.

  Remember: ANDS
  Accelerate
  North
  Decelerate
  South

  Northerly turning error—The compass leads in the south half of a turn, and lags in the north half of a turn.

(continued)

Chapter 3 **Ground Instruction Requirement**

Remember: UNOS
U ndershoot
N orth
O vershoot
S outh

[FAA-H-8083-15]

2. What does the term automation management refer to?

Automation management is the demonstrated ability to control and navigate an aircraft by means of the automated systems installed in the aircraft. It includes understanding whether and when to use automated systems, including, but not limited to, the GPS and the autopilot.

[FAA-H-8083-2]

3. In what three areas must a pilot be proficient when using advanced avionics or any automated system?

The pilot must know what to expect, how to monitor the system for proper operation, and be prepared to promptly take appropriate action if the system does not perform as expected.

[FAA-H-8083-25]

4. What is the most important aspect of managing an autopilot/FMS?

Knowing at all times which modes are engaged, which modes are armed to engage, and being capable of verifying that armed functions (e.g. navigation tracking or altitude capture) engage at the appropriate time.

[FAA-H-8083-2]

5. At a minimum, the pilot flying with advanced avionics must know how to manage what three primary items?

The course deviation indicator (CDI), the navigation source, and the autopilot.

[FAA-H-8083-25]

6. Automation management is a good place to practice the standard callout technique. What are standard callouts?

To assist in maintaining situational awareness, professional flight crews often use standard callouts. For example, the non-flying pilot may call 2,000 and 1,000 feet prior to reaching an assigned altitude. The callout may be, "two to go," then "one to go." Single pilot operations can also benefit from this practice by adopting standard set callouts that can be used in the different segments of a flight. Examples of standard callouts are: "power set," "airspeed alive," "rotate," "positive rate—gear up," "localizer alive," "glideslope alive," "nav source verified," "approach mode armed," "approach mode active," "final approach fix," etc.

[FAA-H-8083-16]

7. When flying a technically advanced aircraft (TAA), what are several procedures that help ensure that situational awareness is enhanced, not diminished, by automation?

Two basic procedures are to always double-check the system and to use verbal callouts. At a minimum, ensure the presentation makes sense. Was the correct destination fed into the navigation system? Callouts, even for single-pilot operations, are an excellent way to maintain situational awareness as well as manage information.

[FAA-H-8083-25]

8. What additional procedures can be used for maintaining situational awareness in technically advanced aircraft?

a. Perform verification checks of all programming prior to departure.

b. Check the flight routing—ensure all routing matches the planned route of flight.

c. Always verify waypoints.

d. Make use of all onboard navigation equipment—use VOR to backup GPS, and vice versa.

e. Match the use of the automated system with pilot proficiency—stay within personal limitations.

(continued)

Chapter 3 **Ground Instruction Requirement**

    f. Plan a realistic flight route to maintain situational awareness—ATC doesn't always give you direct routing.

    g. Be ready to verify computer data entries—incorrect keystrokes can lead to loss of situational awareness.

[FAA-H-8083-25]

Y. Human Factors

1. What factors can make a pilot more susceptible to hypoxia?

The altitude at which significant effects of hypoxia occur can be lowered by a number of factors. Carbon monoxide inhaled in smoking or from exhaust fumes, lowered hemoglobin (anemia), and certain medications can reduce the oxygen-carrying capacity of the blood. Small amounts of alcohol and low doses of certain drugs, such as antihistamines, tranquilizers, sedatives, and analgesics can, through their depressant action, render the brain much more susceptible to hypoxia. Extreme heat and cold, fever, and anxiety increase the body's demand for oxygen, and hence its susceptibility to hypoxia.

[AIM 8-1-2]

2. What symptoms can a pilot expect from hyperventilation?

As hyperventilation blows off excessive carbon dioxide from the body, a pilot can experience symptoms of lightheadedness, suffocation, drowsiness, tingling in the extremities, and coolness, and react to them with even greater hyperventilation. Incapacitation can eventually result from uncoordination, disorientation, and painful muscle spasms. Finally, unconsciousness can occur.

[AIM 8-1-3]

Chapter 3 Ground Instruction Requirement

3. How does carbon monoxide poisoning occur and for what symptoms should a pilot be alert?

Most heaters in light aircraft work by air flowing over the manifold. The use of these heaters while exhaust fumes are escaping through manifold cracks and seals is responsible every year for several nonfatal and fatal aircraft accidents from carbon monoxide poisoning. A pilot who detects the odor of exhaust or experiences symptoms of headache, drowsiness, or dizziness while using the heater should suspect carbon monoxide poisoning.

[AIM 8-1-4]

4. What method does the FAA encourage pilots to use as a logical way to approach decision making?

The DECIDE Model is a six-step, continuous-loop decision-making process which can be used to assist a pilot when they are faced with a situation requiring judgment:

Detect—the decisionmaker detects the fact that change has occurred.

Estimate—the decisionmaker estimates the need to counter or react to the change.

Choose—the decisionmaker chooses a desirable outcome (in terms of success for the flight).

Identify—the decisionmaker identifies actions that could successfully control the change.

Do—the decisionmaker takes the necessary action.

Evaluate—the decisionmaker evaluates the effect(s) of his/her action countering the change.

[FAA-H-8083-2]

Chapter 3 Ground Instruction Requirement

5. What are the 5 types of hazardous attitudes the FAA has identified and provided antidotes for, to encourage pilots to develop a realistic perspective on attitudes toward flying?

Antiauthority (Don't tell me!) — Follow the rules, they are usually right.

Impulsivity (Do something quickly!) — Not so fast. Think first.

Invulnerability (It won't happen to me.) — It could happen to me.

Macho (I can do it) — Taking chances is foolish.

Resignation (What's the use?) — I'm not helpless, I can make a difference.

[FAA-H-8083-2]

6. Define the term *risk management*.

Risk management is a decision-making process designed to systematically identify hazards, assess the degree of risk, and determine the best course of action. It is a logical process of weighing the potential costs of risks against the possible benefits of allowing those risks to stand uncontrolled.

[FAA-H-8083-2]

7. How can the use of the PAVE checklist during flight planning help you to assess risk?

Use of the PAVE checklist provides pilots with a simple way to remember each category to examine for risk during flight planning. The pilot divides the risks of flight into four categories:

Pilot-In-Command — general health, physical/mental/emotional state, proficiency, currency.

Aircraft — airworthiness, equipment, performance capability.

enVironment — weather hazards, terrain, airports/runways to be used, conditions.

External pressures — meetings, people waiting at destination, desire to impress someone, etc.

[FAA-H-8083-2]

Chapter 3 Ground Instruction Requirement

8. **Explain the use of a personal minimums checklist and how it can help a pilot control risk.**

    One of the most important concepts that safe pilots understand is the difference between what is legal in terms of the regulations, and what is smart or safe in terms of pilot experience and proficiency. One way a pilot can control the risks is to set personal minimums for items in each risk category. These are limits unique to that individual pilot's current level of experience and proficiency.

    [FAA-H-8083-2, FAA Safety]

9. **Define the term *task management*.**

    Task management is the process by which pilots manage the many, concurrent tasks that must be performed to safely and efficiently operate an aircraft.

    [FAA-H-8083-2]

10. **What are the different tasks that task management may consist of at any given time?**

    a. *Initiation* of new tasks.

    b. *Monitoring* of ongoing tasks to determine their status.

    c. *Prioritization* of tasks based on importance, status, urgency, and other factors.

    d. *Allocation* of human and machine resources to high-priority tasks.

    e. *Interruption* and subsequent resumption of lower priority tasks.

    f. *Termination* of tasks that have been completed or are no longer relevant.

    [FAA-H-8083-2]

Chapter 3 **Ground Instruction Requirement**

11. What are several options that a pilot can employ to decrease workload and avoid becoming overloaded?

Stop, think, slow down, and prioritize. Tasks such as locating an item on a chart or setting a radio frequency may be delegated to another pilot or passenger; an autopilot, if available, may be used; or ATC may be enlisted to provide assistance.

[FAA-H-8083-25]

12. What is one method of prioritizing tasks to avoid an overload situation?

During any situation, and especially in an emergency, remember the phrase "aviate, navigate, and communicate."

[FAA-H-8083-25]

13. How can tasks be completed in a timely manner without causing a distraction from flying?

By planning, prioritizing, and sequencing tasks, a potential work overload situation can be avoided. As experience is gained, a pilot learns to recognize future workload requirements and can prepare for high workload periods during times of low workload.

[FAA-H-8083-2]

14. Why are pilots encouraged to use checklists?

The checklist is an aid to the memory and helps to ensure that critical items necessary for the safe operation of aircraft are not overlooked or forgotten. They provide a standardized method for verifying aircraft configuration and a logical sequence for accomplishing tasks inside and outside the cockpit.

[FAA-H-8083-3]

15. What are two common methods of checklist usage?

  a. *Do-Verify (DV) method*—consists of the checklist being accomplished in a variable sequence without a preliminary challenge. After all of the action items on the checklist have been completed, the checklist is then read again while each item is verified. The DV method allows the pilot/flightcrew to use flow patterns from memory to accomplish a series of actions quickly and efficiently.

b. *Challenge-Do-Verify (CDV) method*—consists of a pilot/ crewmember making a challenge before an action is initiated, taking the action, and then verifying that the action item has been accomplished. The CDV method is most effective in two-pilot crews where one crewmember issues the challenge and the second crewmember takes the action and responds to the first crewmember, verifying that the action was taken.

[Order 8900.1]

16. What are several examples of common errors that can occur when using a checklist?

a. Checklist items are missed because of distraction or interruption (by passengers, ATC, etc.).
b. Checklist items are incorrectly performed (hurrying checklist; reading item but not verifying or setting).
c. Failure to use the appropriate checklist for a specific phase of flight.
d. Too much time spent with head down, reading the checklist and compromising safety.
e. Checklist is not readily accessible in cockpit.
f. Emergency/abnormal procedures checklist is not readily available.
g. Memory items accomplished but not confirmed with checklist.

17. In what phases of flight should a prepared checklist be used?

a. Preflight inspection.
b. Before engine start.
c. Engine starting.
d. Before taxiing.
e. Before takeoff.
f. After takeoff.
g. Cruise.
h. Descent.
i. Before landing.
j. After landing.
k. Engine shutdown and securing.

[FAA-H-8083-3]

Chapter 3 **Ground Instruction Requirement**

18. What are several recommended methods for managing checklist accomplishment?

   a. The pilot should touch/point at each control, display or switch.

   b. Verbally state the desired status of the checklist item.

   c. When complete, announce that "___ checklist is complete."

   [Order 8900.1]

19. What are immediate action items?

   An immediate action item is an action that must be accomplished so expeditiously (in order to avoid or stabilize a hazardous situation) that time is not available for the pilot/crewmember to refer to a manual or checklist. Once the emergency has been brought under control, the pilot refers to the actual checklist to verify that all immediate action items were accomplished. Only after this is done should the remainder of the checklist be completed.

   [Order 8900.1]

20. Define the term *situational awareness*.

   Situational awareness (SA) is the accurate perception and understanding of all the factors and conditions within the four fundamental risk elements (pilot, aircraft, environment, external pressures) that affect safety before, during, and after the flight.

   [FAA-H-8083-25]

21. What are some of the elements inside and outside the aircraft that a pilot must consider to maintain situational awareness?

   Inside the aircraft—the status of aircraft systems, pilot, and passengers.

   Outside the aircraft—awareness of where the aircraft is in relation to terrain, traffic, weather, and airspace.

   [FAA-H-8083-2]

22. What are several factors that reduce situational awareness?

Factors that reduce SA include fatigue, distractions, unusual or unexpected events, complacency, high workload, unfamiliar situations, and inoperative equipment.

[FAA-H-8083-15]

23. A majority of controlled flight into terrain (CFIT) accidents have been attributed to what factors?

a. Lack of pilot currency.
b. Loss of situational awareness.
c. Pilot distractions and breakdown of SRM.
d. Failure to comply with minimum safe altitudes.
e. Breakdown in effective ADM.
f. Insufficient planning, especially for the descent and arrival segments.

[AC 61-134]

24. A pilot can decrease the likelihood of a CFIT accident at the destination by identifying what risk factors prior to flight?

Factors such as airport location, runway lighting, weather/daylight conditions, approach specifications, ATC capabilities and limitations, type of operation, departure procedures, controller/pilot phraseology, and crew configuration should all be considered prior to flight.

[FAA-H-8083-16]

25. Describe several operational techniques that will help you avoid a CFIT accident.

a. Maintain situational awareness at all times.

b. Adhere to safe takeoff and departure procedures.

c. Familiarize yourself with surrounding terrain features and obstacles.

d. Adhere to published routes and minimum altitudes.

e. Fly a stabilized approach.

f. Understand ATC clearances and instructions.

g. Don't become complacent.

[AC 61-134]

Review: Sample Written Exercise

Candidate Information

Name:
_____

Certificate:
_____

Ratings:
_____

Flight review expiration date: _____
Class of Medical: _____
Medical expiration date: _____

1. A flight review must contain: _____ ground training _____ flight training.

2. The ground portion of the flight review must contain a comprehensive review of Part _____ .

3. The flight portion of the flight review must contain those maneuvers _____ .

4. What flights must be logged in a logbook? _____
_____

5. In order to carry passengers, you must have made _____ landings in the category and class within the previous _____ days.

6. What information must pilots familiarize themselves with before each flight?_____
_____

7. No person may pilot an aircraft within _____ hours of consumption of any alcoholic beverage.

8. What drugs cannot be taken before a flight?_____
_____

Chapter 3 **Ground Instruction Requirement**

9. A parachute is necessary if a pilot is carrying a passenger, if a bank angle of _____ degrees or a nose up or down angle of _____ degrees for any intentional maneuver is exceeded.

10. Fuel reserves for VFR flight are: day _____ night _____ .

11. Where is a transponder (with Mode C) necessary?

    a. _____

    b. _____

    c. _____

    d. _____

    e. _____

12. Oxygen is required above _____ feet regardless of the time flown at that altitude.

13. What three flight instruments are required for this flight?

    a. _____

    b. _____

    c. _____

14. An ELT is required if a training flight goes beyond _____ miles from your departure point and the aircraft is equipped to carry more than one person.

15. When aircraft are approaching head on, each aircraft shall alter their course to the _____ .

16. No person may perform aerobatics below _____ feet.

17. The minimum altitude over a congested area is _____ feet above the highest obstacle within _____ feet horizontally.

18. Two-way radio communications are necessary within Class(es)_____ airspace.

Chapter 3 **Ground Instruction Requirement**

19. The standard pattern at an airport without a control tower and no visual pattern markings is _____-hand turns.

20. Clearance from ATC is necessary to penetrate Class(es) _____ airspace.

21. You may not operate in _____ or _____ areas without permission of the controlling agency.

22. You may not operate in Class A airspace under _____ flight rules.

23. Basic VFR weather minimums in controlled airspace below 10,000 feet are _____ miles visibility and _____ below, _____ above, and _____ horizontally from clouds.

24. VFR minimums in Class G airspace, under 10,000 feet, daytime, are _____ mile(s) visibility and _____ of clouds.

25. Under Special VFR, daytime, you may operate with visibility at least _____ miles and _____ of clouds when cleared by ATC.

26. When is an instrument rating required to operate under Special VFR? _____

27. When operating below 18,000 feet MSL and above 3,000 AGL, you should cruise at _____ thousands plus 500 feet on a mag course of 360 through 179 degrees, and _____ thousands plus 500 feet on a mag course of 180 through 359 degrees.

28. The maximum allowable gross weight for this aircraft is _____ pounds.

29. Our takeoff gross weight is _____ pounds.

30. Our center of gravity is _____ and is within limits (show work).

31. Our fuel minimum for this flight is _____ gallons.

Chapter 3 **Ground Instruction Requirement**

32. Our stall speed in a clean configuration is _____ mph/kts (circle one).
33. You cannot spin the airplane if you keep the nose _____ the horizon and keep the ball _____ .
34. Spin recovery for this airplane requires: _____ .
35. You must always enter the traffic pattern at a 45 degree angle to the downwind. True / False
36. The traffic pattern for this flight should be at _____ feet MSL, and _____ feet AGL.
37. The most important thing to do in the event of engine failure is to maintain _____ speed.
38. What is the meaning of each light signal?

Signal	Air	Ground
Steady Green		
Flashing Green		
Steady Red		
Flashing Red		
Flashing White		
Alternating Red & Green		

Flight Instruction Requirement 4

4 Flight Instruction Requirement

Maneuvers Tables

Although the flight review is *not* a checkride, a review of the Airman Certification Standards (FAA-S-ACS-6) can offer some review into the standards your certificate is based on. These tolerances are not mandatory for a successful flight review, but they do demonstrate safe and skillful flying.

Private Pilot Airman Certification Standards (FAA-S-ACS-6) (condensed)

Task	Objective Minimum acceptable standard of performance			

Takeoff
  Normal/Crosswind
  Short/Soft
	V_Y +10 / -5
	V_X +10 / -5, then V_Y +10 / -5			

Landing
  Normal/Crosswind
  Forward Slip
  Short
  Soft
  Go Around
	1.3 V_{S0} +10 / -5, touch at or within 400 feet beyond target
	Min float, touch at or within 400 feet beyond target
	1.3 V_{S0} +10 / -5, touch at or within 200 feet beyond target
	1.3 V_{S0} +10 / -5, touch at minimum speed and descent rate
	Power (Carb Heat off?), pitch for V_Y +10 / -5, flaps, gear			

Emergency Operations Emergency Approach and Landing	Use recommended descent configuration and airspeed ±10 kts.			
		Heading or bank ±°	Altitude ± ft	Speed ± kts
Traffic Pattern	Accurate track and safe spacing		100	10
Pilotage/NAV/Diverting	Know position ± 3 NM	15	200	ETA ±5min

Instrument Flying
  Straight and level
  Constant airspeed climb and descend
  Turns and rollouts on heading
  Communications, Navigation, Radar Services
  Recovery from unusual attitudes
	
	Recover to stabilized flight w/o excesses
		
		20
		20
		
		10
		20
			
			200
			200
			
			200
			200
				
				10
				10
				
				10
				10

Slow Flight and Stalls (no flight below 1,500 AGL) Power-off Stalls Power-on Stalls Maneuvering during Slow Flight Straight & level, turns, climbs, descents	 S & L or max. 20° bank Full-stall then recover S & L or max. 20° bank Full-stall then recover 	 10 10 10	 100	 Just above stall warning
Performance Maneuvers Steep turns 360° with 45° ±5° bank, coordinated		10	100	10
Ground Reference Maneuvers	Remain 600–1,000 AGL		100	10

4 Flight Instruction Requirement

Commercial Pilot Airman Certification Standards (FAA-S-ACS-7) (condensed)

Task	Objective Minimum acceptable standard of performance			
Takeoff Normal/Crosswind Soft Short	$V_Y \pm 5$ V_X (or mfr's recommended) ± 5, then $V_Y \pm 5$ V_X (or 1.3 V_{S0}) ± 5, -0 then $V_Y \pm 5$			
Landing Normal Short Soft Go Around	± 5 of mfr, touch at or within 200 feet beyond target ± 5 of mfr, touch at or within 100 feet beyond target ± 5 of mfr $V_Y \pm 5$ after power pitch for initial mfr speed, flaps, gear			
Power-off 180° Accuracy Approach & Landing	1,000 feet AGL abeam touchdown point on downwind, power off, touch at or within 200 feet beyond target			
		Heading or bank $\pm °$	Altitude $\pm$ ft	Speed $\pm$ kts
Traffic Pattern	Accurate track and safe spacing		100	10
Slow Flight & Maximum Performance (no flight below 1,500 AGL)				Just above stall warning
STALLS Power on Power off Accelerated	S&L $\pm 5°$, max bank 20° S&L $\pm 10°$, max bank 20° Steady flight, below V_A, 20 kts above unaccel. stall speed	10° bank in turn 5° bank in turn apx 45° bank		
SLOW FLIGHT V_{MCA} Straight & level, turns, climbs, descents		5° bank angle 10° heading	50	MCA +5/-0
STEEP TURN 360° with 50° bank, $\pm 5°$ coordinated		5° bank 10° heading	100	10
STEEP SPIRAL 360° descending turn	60° bank	10° Hdg on rollout	100	10
CHANDELLE Coordinated, positive control		10° Hdg @ 180	50	V_{MCA} on rollout
LAZY EIGHTS Coordinated, positive control, orientation		10° Hdg @ 180	100	10
Ground Reference Maneuvers EIGHTS ON PYLONS	S&L b/w pylons line of sight reference line on pylon, bank 30–40°			
Emergency Approach	Maintain mfr. glide ± 10 kts while using checklist en route best site			

Appendix 1
FAA Guidance Document: *Conducting an Effective Flight Review**

*This and other FAA guidance documents are available at: **www.faasafety.gov**

Appendix 1

Introduction

General aviation (GA) pilots enjoy a level of flexibility and freedom unrivaled by their aeronautical contemporaries. Airline, corporate, and military flight operations are all strictly regulated, and each uses a significant degree of internal oversight to ensure compliance. GA has relatively few of these regulatory encumbrances. As a result, safety depends heavily upon the development and maintenance of each individual pilot's basic skills, systems knowledge, and aeronautical decision-making skills.

The purpose of the flight review required by Title 14 of the Code of Federal Regulations (14 CFR) 61.56 is to provide for a regular evaluation of pilot skills and aeronautical knowledge. AC 61-98 states that the flight review is also intended to offer pilots the opportunity to design a personal currency and proficiency program in consultation with a certificated flight instructor (CFI). In effect, the flight review is the aeronautical equivalent of a regular medical checkup and ongoing health improvement program. Like a physical exam, a flight review may have certain standard features (e.g., review of specific regulations and maneuvers). However, just as the physician should tailor the exam and follow-up to the individual's characteristics and needs, the CFI should tailor both the flight review and any follow-up plan for training and proficiency to each pilot's skill, experience, aircraft, and personal flying goals.

To better accomplish these objectives, this guide, intended for use in conjunction with AC 61-98, offers ideas for conducting an effective flight review. It also provides tools for helping that pilot develop a personalized currency, proficiency, risk management, and aeronautical health maintenance and improvement program. A key part of this process is the development of risk management strategies and realistic personal minimums. You can think of these minimums as individual "operations specifications" that can help guide the pilot's decisions and target areas for personal proficiency flying and future training.

Step 1: Preparation

Managing Expectations: You have probably seen it, or perhaps even experienced it yourself: pilot and CFI check the clock, spend *exactly* one hour reviewing 14 CFR Part 91 operating rules, and then head out for a quick pass through the basic maneuvers generally known as airwork. The pilot departs with a fresh flight review endorsement and, on the basis of the minimum two hours required in 14 CFR 61.56, can legally operate for the next two years. This kind of flight review may be adequate for some pilots, but for others — especially those who do not fly on a regular basis — it is not. To serve the aviation safety purpose for which it was intended, therefore, the flight review must be far more than an exercise in watching the clock and checking the box.

AC 61-98 states that the flight review is "an instructional service designed to assess a pilot's knowledge and skills." The regulations are even more specific: 14 CFR 61.56 states that the person giving the flight review has the discretion to determine the maneuvers and procedures necessary for the pilot to demonstrate "safe exercise of the privileges of the pilot certificate." It is thus a proficiency-based exercise, and it is up to you, the instructional service provider, to determine how much time and what type of instruction is required to ensure that the pilot has the necessary knowledge and skills for safe operation.

Managing pilot expectations is key to ensuring that you don't later feel pressured to conduct a "minimum time" flight review for someone whose aeronautical skills are rusty. When a pilot schedules a flight review, use the Pilot's Aeronautical History for Flight Review form in this Appendix (on Page 157) to find out not only about total time, but also about type of flying (e.g., local leisure flying, or cross-country flying for personal transportation) and recent flight experience. You also need to know if the pilot wants to combine the flight review with a new endorsement or aircraft checkout. Offer an initial estimate of how much time to plan for ground and flight training. How much time is "enough" will vary from pilot to pilot. Someone who flies the same airplane 200 hours every year may not need as much time as someone who has logged only 20 hours since the last flight review, or a pilot seeking a new endorsement in conjunction with the flight review. For pilots who have not flown at all for several years, a useful "rule of thumb" is to plan one hour of ground training and one hour of flight training for every year the pilot has been out of the cockpit. As appropriate, you can also suggest time in an aircraft training device (ATD), or a session of night flying for pilots whose activities include flying (especially VFR) after dark.

In preparation for the flight review session, give the pilot two assignments.

Review of Part 91: The regulations (14 CFR 61.56) state that the flight review must include a review of the current general operating and flight rules set out in Part 91. The *Aeronautical Information Manual* (AIM) also contains information that pilots need to know. Have the pilot complete the Flight Review Preparation Course now available in the Aviation Learning Center at **faasafety.gov** in advance of your session and bring a copy of the completion certificate to the flight review. The online course lets the pilot review material at his or her own pace and focus attention on areas of particular interest. Alternatively, provide a copy of the Regulatory Review Guide (starting on Page 158) as a self-study guide.

Cross-Country Flight Plan Assignment: Many people learn to fly for personal transportation, but the cross-country flight planning skills learned for practical test purposes can become rusty if they are not used on a regular basis. Structuring the flight review as a short cross-country (i.e., 30–50 miles from the home airport) is an excellent way to refresh the pilot's flight planning skills. Ask the pilot to plan a VFR cross-country to another airport, ideally one that they have not

previously visited. Be sure to specify that the flight plan should include consideration of runway lengths, weather, expected aircraft performance, alternatives, length of runways to be used, traffic delays, fuel requirements, terrain avoidance strategies, and NOTAM/TFR information. The *GA Pilot's Guide to Preflight Weather Planning, Weather Self-Briefings, and Weather Decision-Making* may be of help to the pilot in this part of the exercise. Proficiency in weight and balance calculations is critical as well. If the pilot regularly flies with passengers, consider asking for calculations based on maximum gross weight.

It is within your discretion to require a "manual" flight plan created with a sectional chart, plotter, and E6-B. In real-world flying, however, many pilots today use online flight planning software for basic information and calculations. Appropriate use of these tools can enhance safety in several ways: they provide precise course and heading information; the convenience may encourage more consistent use of a flight plan; and automating manual calculations leaves more time to consider weather, performance, terrain, alternatives, and other aspects of the flight. Encouraging the pilot to use his or her preferred online tool will give you a more realistic picture of real-world behavior, and the computer-generated plan will give you an excellent opportunity to point out both the advantages and the potential pitfalls of this method.

Appendix 1

Step 2: Ground Review

The regulations (14 CFR 61.56) specify only that the ground portion of the flight review must include "a review of the current general operating and flight rules of Part 91." This section offers guidance on conducting that review. It also provides guidance on additional topics that you should address. These include:

- Review and discussion of the pre-assigned cross-country (XC) flight plan, with special emphasis on weather and weather decision-making; risk management and individual personal minimums; and
- General aviation security (TFRs, aircraft security, and airport security).

Regulatory Review. Since most GA pilots do not read rules on a regular basis, this review is an important way to refresh the pilot's knowledge of information critical to aviation safety, as well as to ensure that they stay up-to-date on changes since the last flight review or formal aviation training session. If the pilot has completed the online flight review course in advance, you will want to review the results and focus primarily on those questions the pilot answered incorrectly. If the pilot has done nothing to prepare, the "Regulatory Review Guide" (*see* Page 158) is one way to guide your discussion. You might also organize the rules as they relate to the pre-assigned cross-country flight plan that you will discuss. The important thing is to put the rules and operating procedures into a context that is relevant and meaningful to the pilot, as opposed to the sequential approach that encourages rote memorization rather than higher levels of understanding.

XC Flight Plan Review: At the most basic level, you are reviewing the pre-assigned flight plan for accuracy and completeness (i.e., are the calculations correct? Did the pilot show understanding of the 14 CFR 91.103 requirement to become familiar with "all" available information?) You may want to use the "Pilot's Cross-Country Checklist" as a guide for checking the completeness of the pre-assigned plan.

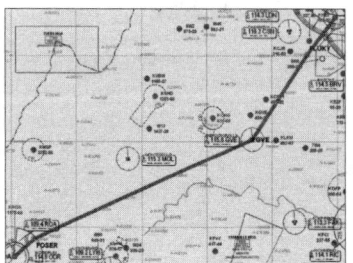

If the pilot used automated tools to develop the flight plan, here are some questions and issues that you should teach them to ask about the computer-generated package:

- How do I know that the computer-generated information is correct? (*Not all online flight planning and flight information tools are the same. Some provide real-time updates; others may be as dangerous as an out-of-date chart.*)
- Does the computer-generated information pass the "common sense" test? (*Garbage-in, garbage-out is a fundamental principle in any kind of automation. If a pilot headed for Augusta, Georgia (KAGS) mistakenly asks for KAUG, the resulting flight plan will go to Augusta, Maine instead.*)
- Does this plan include all the information I am required to consider? (*Some planning tools compute only course and distance, without regard to wind, terrain, performance, and other factors in a safety-focused flight plan*).
- Does this plan keep me out of trouble? (*What if the computer-proposed course takes you through high terrain in high density altitude conditions?*)
- What will I do if I cannot complete the flight according to this plan? (*Weather can always interfere, but pilots should also understand that flight planning software does not always generate ATC-preferred routes for IFR flying.*)

Each of these questions is directed to a critical point that you should emphasize: automated flight planning tools can be enormously helpful, but the pilot must *always* review the information with a critical eye, *frequently* supplement the computer's plan with additional information, and *never* simply assume that the computer-generated package "must be" okay because the machine is smarter.

Asking these kinds of questions is key to critical thinking, which is in turn the secret to good aeronautical decision-making (ADM) and risk management. There are many models for ADM, including charts that provide quantitative assessment and generate a numerical "score" that pilots can use in evaluating the level of risk. Although these tools can be useful, you may want to present the "3–P" method developed by the FAA Aviation Safety Program. This model encourages the pilot to **P**erceive hazards, **P**rocess risk level, and **P**erform risk management by asking a series of questions about various aspects of the flight. The "3–P Risk Management Process" explains this method in detail.

Appendix 1

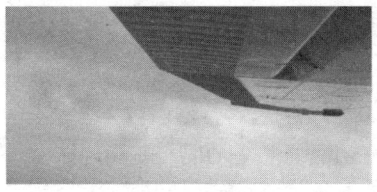

Since statistics show that weather is still the factor most likely to result in accidents with fatalities, the XC flight plan assignment also provides an important opportunity to discuss weather and weather decision-making. The *GA Pilot's Guide to Preflight Weather Planning, Weather Self-Briefings, and Weather Decision-Making*, which uses the 3–P method as a framework for weather decision-making, might be helpful in this discussion. If the pilot flies VFR at night, be sure to talk about night flying considerations, especially in overcast or "no moon" conditions.

GA Security: In the post-September 11 security environment, any security incident involving general aviation pilots, aircraft, and airports can prompt calls for new restrictions. As a flight instructor, you have a special responsibility to ensure that your clients know and follow basic security procedures. These include not only respect for temporary flight restrictions (TFRs), but also for the importance of securing your aircraft against unauthorized use. Pilots should never leave the aircraft unlocked or, worse, unattended with the keys inside.

In addition, be sure that the pilot knows about the Airport Watch Program, which was developed by the Transportation Security Administration (TSA) and the Aircraft Owners and Pilots Association (AOPA). Airport Watch relies upon the nation's pilots to observe and report suspicious activity. The Airport Watch Program is supported by a government-provided toll free hotline (1-866-GA-SECURE) and system for reporting and acting on information provided by general aviation pilots. A General Aviation Security checklist of what to look for is included in this Appendix (on Page 162). For more information on GA security, see TSA's GA security website and AOPA's online GA security resources page.

For specific information on flying in security-restricted airspace, including the Washington DC metropolitan area Air Defense Identification Zone (ADIZ), direct pilots to the FAA's new online ADIZ–TFR training course and to the Air Safety Foundation's online airspace training courses.

Step 3: Flight Activities

To operate safely in the modern flight environment, the pilot needs solid skills in three distinct, but interrelated, areas. These include:

"Physical Airplane" Skills
(i.e., basic stick-and-rudder proficiency);

"Mental Airplane" Skills
(i.e., knowledge and proficiency in aircraft systems);

Aeronautical Decision-Making (ADM) Skills (i.e., higher-order thinking skills).

Many flight reviews consist almost exclusively of airwork followed by multiple takeoffs and landings. These maneuvers can give you a very good snapshot of the pilot's "physical airplane" skills. They are also good for the pilot, who gets a safe opportunity to practice proficiency maneuvers that they may not have performed since the last flight review. Airwork alone, however, will tell you little about the pilot's "mental airplane" knowledge of avionics and other aircraft systems, and even less about the pilot's ability to make safe and appropriate decisions in real-world flying (ADM). Therefore, you need to structure the exercise to give you a clear picture of the pilot's skills with respect to each area.

Having the pilot fly the cross-country trip you assigned and discussed in the ground review is a good way to achieve this goal. One leg will involve flying from departure to destination, during which you ensure that the pilot encounters scenarios that let you evaluate the pilot's systems knowledge ("mental airplane") and decision-making skills, including risk management. The other leg (which can come first, depending on how you choose to organize the exercise) will focus more on airwork, which allows you to evaluate "physical airplane" skills.

Appendix 1

Be sure to include a diversion. Remember the computer-generated flight plan discussed during the ground review portion? While you are en route to the planned destination, give the pilot a scenario that requires an  immediate diversion (e.g., mechanical problem, unexpected weather). Ask the pilot to choose an alternate destination and, using all available and appropriate resources (e.g., chart, basic rules of thumb, "nearest" and "direct to" functions on the GPS) to calculate the approximate course, heading, distance, and time needed to reach the new destination. Proceed to that point and, if at all feasible, do some of the "physical airplane" pattern work at the unexpected alternate.

The diversion exercise has several benefits. First, it generates "teachable moments," which are defined as those times when the learner is most aware of the need for certain information or skills, and therefore most receptive to learning what you want to teach. Diverting to an airport surrounded by high terrain, for example, provides a "teachable moment" on the importance of obstacle awareness and terrain avoidance planning. Second, the diversion exercise quickly and efficiently reveals the pilot's level of skill in each of the three areas:

- *"Physical Airplane" Skills:* Does the pilot maintain control of the aircraft when faced with a major distraction? For a satisfactory flight review, the pilot should be able to perform all maneuvers in accordance with the Practical Test Standards (PTS) for the pilot certificate that they hold.

- *"Mental Airplane" Skills:* Does the pilot demonstrate knowledge and proficiency in using avionics, aircraft systems, and "bring-your-own-panel" handheld devices? Since many GA pilots use handheld GPS navigators, you will want to see whether the pilot can safely and appropriately operate the devices that will be used when you are not on board to monitor and serve as the ultimate safety net. Appropriate and proficient use of the autopilot is another "mental airplane" skill to evaluate in this exercise.

- *Aeronautical Decision-Making (ADM) Skills:* Give the pilot multiple opportunities to make decisions. Asking questions about those decisions is an excellent way to get the information you need to evaluate ADM skills, including risk management. For example, ask the pilot to explain why the alternate airport selected for the diversion exercise is a safe and appropriate choice. What are the possible hazards, and what can the pilot do to mitigate them? Be alert to the pilot's information and automation management skills as well. For example, does the pilot perform regular "common sense cross-checks" of what the GPS and/or the autopilot are doing?

Appendix 1

Step 4: Postflight Debriefing

Most instructors have experienced the traditional "sage on the stage" model of training, in which the teacher does all the talking and hands out grades with little or no student input. There is a place for this kind of debriefing; however, a collaborative critique is one of the most effective ways to determine that the pilot has not only the physical and mental airplane skills, but also the self-awareness and judgment needed for sound aeronautical decision-making. Here is one way to structure a collaborative post flight critique:

Replay: Rather than starting the post flight briefing with a laundry list of areas for improvement, ask the pilot to verbally *replay* the flight for you. Listen for areas where your perceptions are different, and explore why they don't match. This approach gives the pilot a chance to validate his or her own perceptions, and it gives you critical insight into his or her judgment abilities.

Reconstruct: The reconstruct stage encourages the pilot to learn by identifying the "would'a could'a should'a" elements of the flight—that is, the key things that they *would have, could have,* or *should have* done differently.

Reflect: Insights come from investing perceptions and experiences with meaning, which in turn requires reflection on these events. For example:

- What was the most important thing you learned today?
- What part of the session was easiest for you? What part was hardest?
- Did anything make you uncomfortable? If so, when did it occur?
- How would you assess your performance and your decisions?
- Did you perform in accordance with the Practical Test Standards?

Appendix 1

Redirect: The final step is to help the pilot relate lessons learned in this flight to other experiences, and consider how they might help in future flights. Questions:
- How does this experience relate to previous flights?
- What might you do to mitigate a similar risk in a future flight?
- Which aspects of this experience might apply to future flights, and how?
- What personal minimums should you establish, and what additional proficiency flying and training might be useful?

Appendix 1

Step 5: Aeronautical Health Maintenance and Improvement

If the pilot did not perform well enough for you to endorse them for satisfactory completion of the flight review, use the PTS as the objective standard to discuss areas needing improvement, as well as areas where the pilot performed well. Offer a practical course of action—ground training, flight training, or both—to help them get back up to standards. If possible, offer to schedule the next session before the pilot leaves the airport.

If the pilot's performance on both ground and flight portions was satisfactory, you can complete the flight review simply by endorsing the pilot's logbook. However, offer the pilot an opportunity to develop a personalized aeronautical health maintenance and improvement plan. Such a plan should include consideration of the following elements:

Personal minimums checklist: One of the most important concepts to convey in the flight review is that safe pilots understand the difference between what is legal in terms of the regulations, and what is smart in terms of pilot experience and proficiency. For this reason, assistance in completing a personal minimums checklist tailored to the pilot's individual circumstances is perhaps the single most important takeaway item you can offer. Use the Personal Minimums Development Worksheet to help your client work through some of the questions that should be considered in establishing hard personal minimums, as well as in preflight and inflight decision making.

Personal proficiency practice plan: Flying just for fun is one of the most wonderful benefits of being a pilot, but many pilots would appreciate your help in developing a plan for maintaining and improving basic aeronautical skills. You might use the suggested flight profile in this Appendix as a guide for developing a regular practice plan.

Training plan: Discuss and schedule any additional training the pilot may need to achieve individual flying goals. For example, the pilot's goal might be to develop the competence and confidence needed to fly at night, or to lower personal minimums in one or more areas. Another goal might be completion of another phase in the FAA's Pilot Proficiency (**WINGS**) Program, or obtaining a complex, high

Appendix 1

performance, or tailwheel endorsement. Use the Personal Aeronautical Goals form on Page 171 to document the pilot's aeronautical goals and develop a specific training plan to help them achieve their goals.

The flight review is vital link in the general aviation safety chain. As a person authorized to conduct this review, you play a critical role in ensuring that it is a meaningful and effective tool for maintaining and enhancing GA safety.

Appendix 1

CFI's Flight Review Checklist

Step 1: Preflight Review Actions
- ☐ Scheduling
- ☐ Pilot's Aeronautical History
- ☐ Part 91 Review Assignment
- ☐ Cross-Country Flight Plan Assignment

Step 2: Ground Discussion
- ☐ Regulatory Review
- ☐ Cross-Country Flight Plan Review
- ☐ Risk Management and Personal Minimums

Step 3: Conducting the Flight
- ☐ Physical Airplane (basic skills)
- ☐ Mental Airplane (systems knowledge)
- ☐ Aeronautical Decision-Making

Step 4: Postflight Discussion
- ☐ Replay, Reflect, Reconstruct, Redirect
- ☐ Questions

Step 5: Aeronautical Health Maintenance and Improvement Plan
- ☐ Personal Minimums Checklist
- ☐ Personal Proficiency Practice Plan
- ☐ Training Plan (if desired)
- ☐ Resources List

Appendix 1

Pilot's Aeronautical History for Flight Review

Pilot's Name: _____ CFI: _____
Address: _____
Phone(s): _____ e-mail: _____

Type of Pilot Certificate(s):
Private _____ Commercial _____ ATP _____ Flight Instructor _____

Rating(s):
Instrument _____ Multiengine _____

Experience (Pilot):
Total time _____ Last 6 months _____ Avg hours/month _____
Time logged since last flight review _____ Since last IPC _____

Experience (Aircraft):
Aircraft type(s) you fly _____
_____

Aircraft used most often _____
For this aircraft:
Total time _____ Last 6 months _____ Avg hours/month _____

Experience (Flight environment):
Since your last flight review, approximately how many hours have you logged in:
Day VFR _____ Day IFR _____ IMC _____
Night VFR _____ Night IFR _____
Mountainous terrain _____ Overwater flying _____
Airport with control tower _____ Airport w/o control tower _____

Type of Flying (External factors):
What percentage of your flying is for:
Pleasure _____ Business _____ Local _____ XC _____

Personal Skills Assessment:
What are your strengths as a pilot? _____
What do you most want to practice/improve? _____
What are your aviation goals? _____

Appendix 1

Regulatory Review Guide

Pilot	**Experience** 　Recent flight experience (61.57) **Responsibility** 　Authority (91.3) 　ATC Instructions (91.123) 　Preflight action (91.103) 　Safety belts (91.107) 　Flight crew at station (91.105) **Cautions** 　Careless or reckless operation (91.13) 　Dropping objects (91.15) 　Alcohol or drugs (91.17 　Supplemental oxygen (91.211) 　Fitness for flight (AIM Chapter 8, Section 1)
Aircraft	**Airworthiness** 　Basic (91.7) 　Flight manual, markings, placards (91.9) 　Certifications required (91.203) 　Instrument and equipment requirements (91.205) 　　–ELT (91.207) 　　–Position lights (91.209) 　　–Transponder requirements (91.215) 　　–Inoperative instruments and equipment (91.213) **Maintenance** 　Responsibility (91.403) 　Maintenance required (91.405) 　Maintenance records (91.417) 　Operation after maintenance (91.407) **Inspections** 　Annual, Airworthiness Directives, 100-Hour (91.409) 　Altimeter and Pitot Static System (91.411) 　VOR check (91.171) 　Transponder (91.413) 　ELT (91.207)

Appendix 1

Regulatory Review Guide *(continued)*

<table>
<tr>
<td rowspan="2">enVironment</td>
<td>

Airports
  Markings (AIM Chapter 2, Section 3)
  Operations (AIM 4-3; 91.126, 91.125)
  Traffic Patterns (91.126)

Airspace
  Altimeter Settings (91.121; AIM 7-2)
  Minimum Safe Altitudes (91.119, 91.177)
  Cruising Altitudes (91.159, 91.179; AIM 3-1-5)
  Speed Limits (91.117)
  Right of Way (91.113)
  Formation (91.111)
  Types of Airspace (AIM 3)
    –Controlled Airspace (AIM 3-2; 91.135, 91.131, 91.130, 91.129)
    –Class G Airspace (AIM 3-3)
    –Special Use (AIM 3-4; 91.133, 91.137, 91.141, 91.143, 91.145)
  Emergency Air Traffic Rules (91.139; AIM 5-6)

Air Traffic Control and Procedures
  Services (AIM 4-1)
  Radio Communications (AIM 4-2 and P/C Glossary)
  Clearances (AIM 4-4)
  Procedures (AIM 5)

Weather
  Meteorology (AIM 7-1)
  Wake Turbulence (AIM 7-3)

</td>
</tr>
<tr></tr>
<tr>
<td>External pressures</td>
<td>

Personal Minimums Checklist
Risk Management (3–P model)
PTS Special Emphasis Items

</td>
</tr>
</table>

Appendix 1

Pilot's Cross-Country Checklist

Pilot

- ☐ Review Personal Minimums Checklist
    - ☐ Recency (time/practice in last 30 days)
    - ☐ Currency (takeoffs and landings, IFR currency if applicable)
    - ☐ Terrain and airspace (familiarity?)
    - ☐ Health and well-being

Aircraft

- ☐ Overall mechanical condition
- ☐ Avionics and systems
- ☐ Performance calculations
- ☐ Fuel requirements
- ☐ Other equipment

EnVironment

- ☐ Weather
    - ☐ Reports and forecasts
        - ☐ Departure
        - ☐ En route
        - ☐ Destination
    - ☐ Severe weather forecasts?
    - ☐ Weather stability?
    - ☐ Alternate required?
- ☐ Night
    - ☐ Flashlights available
    - ☐ Terrain avoidance plan
- ☐ Airspace
    - ☐ TFRs or other restrictions
    - ☐ COM/NAV equipment requirements
    - ☐ Cruising altitude(s)
- ☐ Terrain
    - ☐ VFR and IFR charts with MSA/MEA altitudes
    - ☐ AOPA/ASF Terrain Avoidance Planning
- ☐ Airports
    - ☐ COM/NAV requirements and frequencies
    - ☐ Runway lengths
    - ☐ Services available

External Pressures

- ☐ Family expectations?
- ☐ Passenger needs/expectations?
- ☐ Weather worries?
- ☐ Prepared for diversion (money, accommodations)?
- ☐ Time pressures (e.g., "must be at work" issues)?

Appendix 1

3-P Risk Management Process

Good aeronautical decision-making includes risk management, a process that systematically identifies hazards, assesses the degree of risk, and determines the best course of action. There are many models for risk management, including charts that generate a numerical "score." Although these tools can be useful, numbers-based tools suggest a level of precision that may be misleading.

An alternative method is the Perceive – Process – Perform risk management and aeronautical decision-making model developed by the FAA Aviation Safety Program. There are three basic steps in this model:

PERCEIVE hazards

PROCESS to evaluate level of risk

PERFORM risk management

PERCEIVE: The goal is to identify hazards, which are events, objects, or circumstances that could contribute to an undesired event. You need to consider hazards associated with:

Pilot
Aircraft
en**V**ironment
External Pressures.

PROCESS: Ask questions to determine what can hurt you. In short, why do you have to **CARE** about these hazards?

What are the **C**onsequences?

What are the **A**lternatives available to me?

What is the **R**eality of the situation facing me?

What kind of **E**xternal pressures may affect my thinking?

PERFORM: Change the situation in your favor. Your objective is to make sure the hazard does not hurt *me* or my loved ones, so work to either

Mitigate the risk involved, or

Eliminate the risk involved.

Appendix 1

General Aviation Security

The Transportation Security Administration (TSA) has partnered with the Aircraft Owners and Pilots Association (AOPA) to develop a nationwide Airport Watch Program that uses the more than 650,000 pilots as eyes and ears for observing and reporting suspicious activity. This partnership helps general aviation keep our airports secure without needless and expensive security requirements. AOPA Airport Watch is supported by a centralized government provided toll free hotline (1-866-GA-SECURE) and system for reporting and acting on information provided by general aviation pilots. The Airport Watch Program includes warning signs for airports, informational literature, and training videotape to educate pilots and airport employees as to how security of their airports and aircraft can be enhanced.

Here's what to look for:

- Pilots who appear under the control of someone else.
- Anyone trying to access an aircraft through force — without keys, using a crowbar or screwdriver.
- Anyone who seems unfamiliar with aviation procedures trying to check out an airplane.
- Anyone who misuses aviation lingo — or seems too eager to use all the lingo
- People or groups who seem determined to keep to themselves.
- Any members of your airport neighborhood who work to avoid contact with you or other airport tenants.
- Anyone who appears to be just loitering, with no specific reason for being there.
- Any out-of-the-ordinary videotaping of aircraft or hangars.
- Aircraft with unusual or obviously unauthorized modifications.
- Dangerous cargo or loads — explosives, chemicals, openly displayed weapons — being loaded into an airplane.
- Anything that strikes you as wrong — listen to your gut instinct, and then follow through.
- Pay special attention to height, weight, and the individual's clothing or other identifiable traits.

Use common sense. Not all these items indicate terrorist activity.
When in doubt, check it out!
Check with airport staff or call the National Response Center
1-866-GA-SECURE!

Appendix 1

Developing Personal Weather Minimums

Note This worksheet was adapted from the
Personal and Weather Risk Assessment Guide (October 2003): **www.faasafety.gov**

Certification, Training, and Experience Summary

Certification	Certificate level (e.g., private, commercial, ATP)	
	Ratings (e.g., instrument, multiengine)	
	Endorsements (e.g., complex, high performance, high altitude)	
Training	Flight review (e.g., certificate, rating, Wings Program)	
	Instrument Proficiency Check	
	Time since checkout in airplane 1	
	Time since checkout in airplane 2	
	Time since checkout in airplane 3	
	Variation in equipment used (e.g., GPS navigators)	
Experience	Total flying time	
	Years flying	
	Hours in previous 12 months	
	Hours in this airplane (or identical model) in last 12 months	
	Landings in last 12 months	
	Night hours in last 12 months	
	Night landings in last 12 months	
	Hours flown in high density altitude in last 12 months	
	Hours flown in mountainous terrain in last 12 months	
	Crosswind landings in last 12 months	
	IFR hours in last 12 months	
	IMC hours (actual conditions) in last 12 months	
	Approaches (actual or simulated) in last 12 months	

Note: Use this part of the worksheet to review your recency and currency before a specific flight.

Suggested Personal Minimums

Weather Condition	VFR Pilot (100–200 hours)	IFR Pilot (300–500 hours)	My Personal Minimums
Ceiling & Visibility			
Ceiling–DAY VFR	3,000 feet	2,000 feet	
Ceiling–NIGHT VFR	5,000 feet	3,000 feet	
Ceiling–IFR APPROACH	n/a	Minimums + 500	
Visibility–DAY VFR	5 miles	3 miles	
Visibility–NIGHT VFR	7 miles	5 miles	
Visibility–IFR APPROACH	n/a	Minimums + 1/2 mile	
Turbulence (Wind)			
Surface Wind Speed	15 knots	15 knots	
Surface Wind Gusts	5 knots	5 knots	
Crosswind Component	7 knots	7 knots	
Mountain Flying	Consult instructor or mentor		
Overwater Flying	Consult instructor or mentor		
Icing Conditions	n/a	Consult instructor or mentor	

Appendix 1

PAVE Personal Minimums Development Guide (PILOT Factors)

Pilot's Name: _____ CFI: _____ Date: _____

Example below assumes total time is < 500 hours*; adjust as appropriate for additional experience

		Go	Risk Mitigation Strategy	No-Go
Recency (last 90 days)	>6 TO & LDG	X		
	3–6 TO & LDG	X		
	0–3 TO & LDG		Work with a CFI (especially if total time < 100 hours).	
Time in Type (make & model in last 90 days)	>9	X		
	5–8	X		
	0–4		Work with a CFI (especially if total time < 100 hours).	
IFR App (in last 90 days, if filing IFR)	>3	X		
	<3		Plan practice session in VMC before flying in IMC.	
	0		Work with CFI before filing IFR or flying in IMC.	
IFR Time (in last 90 days, actual or sim)	>3	X		
	<3		Plan practice session in VMC before flying in IMC.	
	0		Work with CFI before filing IFR or flying in IMC.	

*AOPA Air Safety Foundation's Nall Report shows that 32% of all GA accidents and 26% of fatal GA accidents involve pilots with total time under 500 hours.

Appendix 1

PAVE Personal Minimums Development Guide (PILOT Factors) *continued*

Physical Condition

		Go	Risk Mitigation Strategy	No-Go
Sleep (last 24 hours)	>6 hours	X		
	5–6 hours		Fly earlier in the day; avoid night flying.	
	< 5 hours			X
Food & Water	3 meals	X		
	Missed meals?		Take time for meal (or light snack/water) before flight; otherwise – NO-GO.	
Alcohol (last 8 hours)	0	X		
	Any amount			X
Drugs/Meds	0	X		
	Prescription?		Confirm that prescription meds are acceptable to FAA.	
	Other?		Do not fly if under the influence of any drug.	
Stress	Any?		Stress from family, work, or other areas can be a dangerous distraction.	X
Illness	Any?		Do not fly if you are sick – even common colds can be distracting.	X

Appendix 1

PAVE Personal Minimums Development Guide (AIRCRAFT Factors)

Pilot's Name: _____ CFI: _____ Date: _____

Performance		Go	Risk Mitigation Strategy	No-Go
Fuel Reserves (day VFR)	> 1.5 hours	X		
	1 hour	X		
	< 1 hour			X
Fuel Reserves (night VFR)	> 2 hours	X		
	1.5 – 2 hours		Stay within easy range of airport with fuel available at night.	
	< 1.5 hours			X
Fuel Reserves (day or night IFR)	> 2 hour	X		
	< 2 hours			X
Hours (TO & LDGs in type in last 90 days)	3–6	X		
	< 3		Work with a CFI (especially if total time < 100 hours).	
Weight	> MGTOW			X
	< MGTOW	X	If final calculation is close to MGTOW, use precise weights to ensure accuracy.	
CG	In CG range	X		
	Out of CG		Do not operate outside of CG range – redistribute load or do not go!	X
Density Altitude	0–2000	X		
	2000–5000		Carefully calculate performance numbers: TO & LDG, Climb, Cruise.	
	> 5000		Carefully calculate performance; if unaccustomed to high DA ops, do not go!	X
TO & LDG Margins (relative to POH numbers)	> 1000+	X		
	500–1000+		Carefully calculate performance with special attention to chart notes.	
	< 500+			X
Equipment	Avionics		Proficient in operation of all systems?	
	Comm/Nav			
	Charts		Lack of current & appropriate charts is a no-go item!	
	Clothing		Suitable for preflight and enroute conditions.	
	Survival gear		Must have if flying over water, snow, mountains, etc.	

Appendix 1

PAVE Personal Minimums Development Guide (ENVIRONMENT Factors)

Pilot's Name: _____ CFI: _____ Date: _____

Airport Conditions (departure & destination)

		Go	Risk Mitigation Strategy	No-Go
X-Wind (assumes max demonstrated XW of 15 knots)	< 5	X	Are you current and proficient in crosswind landings? Work with CFI.	
	5–10			
	> 10			X
Runway Length (relative to POH numbers)	> 1000+	X	Carefully calculate performance with special attention to chart notes.	
	500–1000+			
	< 500+			X

Weather Conditions (reports & forecasts)

		Go	Risk Mitigation Strategy	No-Go
Reports (METARS, etc.)	< 1 hour old	X	Be especially cautious if there are changes (e.g., SPECI reports).	
	1–3 hours old		Get updated weather before departing.	
	> 3 hours old		Do not operate on basis of reports more than 3 hours old.	X
Forecasts (TAFs, etc.)	< 2 hours old	X	Be suspicious – especially if TAFs have been amended.	
	2–4 hours old		TAFs are produced for 00Z, 06Z, 12Z, and 18Z. Don't use a "stale" forecast!	X
	4–6 hours old			X
Icing	Any		Unless you are qualified and your aircraft is certified for flight into known icing, do not attempt to operate light aircraft in forecast icing conditions.	X
T-Storms	Any		Unless you are qualified and your aircraft has thunderstorm avoidance equipment (radar, stormscope, datalink), do not enter clouds when thunderstorms are forecast. If VFR, do not operate unless you can maintain at least 20 nm away from cumulonimbus.	X

Weather Conditions (ceiling & visibility for day VFR)

		Go	Risk Mitigation Strategy	No-Go
Ceiling	> 3000	X	Ensure that you are current, proficient, and familiar with surrounding terrain.	
	1000–3000			
	< 1000		Not legal for VFR.	X
Visibility	> 5	X	Ensure that you are current, proficient, and familiar with surrounding terrain.	
	5		Although legal for VFR, visibility lower than 5 miles creates a higher risk.	
	< 5			X

Appendix 1

PAVE Personal Minimums Development Guide (ENVIRONMENT Factors) *continued*

Weather Conditions (ceiling & visibility for night VFR)

		Go	Risk Mitigation Strategy	No-Go
Ceiling	>3000	X		
	1000–3000		Terrain considerations are a major factor in the go/no-go decision.	
	<1000		Not legal for VFR.	
Visibility	>5	X		
	5		Visibility below 5 miles creates a higher risk, especially at night	X
	<5			X
Light	Full moon	X		
	>1/4 moon	X		
	No moon or overcast		Fly IFR or do not go – a large majority of fatal night accidents occur when there is an overcast or no moon.	X

Weather Conditions (ceiling & visibility for IFR)

		Go	Risk Mitigation Strategy	No-Go
Ceiling (relative to IAP minimums)	>1000	X		
	500–1000	X		
	minimums		Consider not attempting in single pilot IMC operations.	X
Visibility (relative to IAP minimums)	>2 miles	X	Unless you are current and proficient in IFR procedures and IMC conditions, do not attempt an instrument departure or approach to minimums.	
	1–2 miles+	X		
	<1 mile		Unless you are current and proficient in IFR procedures and IMC conditions, do not attempt an instrument departure or approach with less than 1 mile visibility.	

Factors to Consider in Number of Instrument Approach Attempts

Approach Attempts (at same airport)		Go	Risk Mitigation Strategy	No-Go
	Total IFR time		Regardless of total time, do not attempt more than 2 approaches.	
	IFR experience in last 90 days		Regardless of recent experience, do not attempt more than 2 approaches.	

Appendix 1

PAVE Personal Minimums Development Guide (EXTERNAL PRESSURES)

Pilot's Name: _____ CFI: _____ Date: _____

Trip Planning Considerations

		Go	Risk Mitigation Strategy	No-Go
Tolerance for Delay	> 2 day	X		
	1–2 days	X	Be ready for changes in weather that might require a change in your plans	
	0			X
Available Alternatives for	Passengers		Do not fly if you are under pressure to meet someone else's schedule, unless you have alternative arrangements in place to mitigate the risk.	
	Waiting family			
	Accommodations			
	Alternative transport			
Equipment	Credit cards			
	Money			
	Prescription meds			
	Clothing			

Personal Trip Planning Matrix

PURPOSE of TRIP		Self	Passenger(s)	Family/Friends/Colleagues at Destination	Risk Mitigation Strategies
Tolerance for Delay	> 2 day				
	1–2 days				
	0				
Available Alternatives	Accommodations				
	Transport				
	Meals				
	Other?				
Equipment	Money				
	Credit cards				
	Prescription meds				
	Appropriate clothing				

Appendix 1

Personal Proficiency Practice Plan

Pilot's Name: _____ CFI: _____

Date: _____ Review Date: _____

VFR Flight Profile—Every 4 to 6 Weeks

Preflight (include 3–P Risk Management Process)

Normal taxi, takeoff, departure to practice area.

CHAPS (before each maneuver):

> **C**lear the area
>
> **H**eading established and noted
>
> **A**ltitude established (at least 3,000 AGL)
>
> **P**osition near a suitable emergency landing area
>
> **S**et power and aircraft configuration

Steep turns (both directions), maintaining altitude within 100 feet and airspeed within 10 knots.

Power-off stalls (approach to landing) and recovery.

Power-on stalls (takeoff/departure) and recovery.

Ground reference maneuvers.

Pattern practice:

> Normal landing (full flaps)
>
> Short-field takeoff and landing over a 50-foot obstacle
>
> Soft-field takeoff and landing

Secure the aircraft.

Review your performance.

Schedule next proficiency flight.

Appendix 1

Personal Aeronautical Goals

Pilot's Name: _____ CFI: _____

Date: _____ Review Date: _____

Training Goals

_____ Certificate Level (Private, Commercial, ATP)

_____ Ratings (Instrument, AMEL, ASES, AMES, etc.)

_____ Endorsements (high performance, complex, tailwheel, high altitude)

_____ Phase in Pilot Proficiency (***WINGS***) Program

_____ Instructor Qualifications (CFI, CFI-I, MEI, AGI, IGI)

Other: _____

_____

Proficiency Goals

_____ Lower personal minimums to:

                _____ Ceiling

                _____ Visibility

                _____ Winds

                _____ Precision Approach Minimums

                _____ Non-Precision Approach Minimums

_____ Fly at least:

                _____ Times per month

                _____ Hours per month

                _____ Hours per year

                _____ XC flights per year

                _____ Night hours per month

_____ Make a XC trip to: _____

Other: _____

_____

Aeronautical Training Plan

_____

_____

_____

Appendix 1

Acknowledgements

This guide has been developed with assistance, contributions, and suggestions from a number of general aviation pilots and flight instructors. Special thanks are due to Pat Cannon, Turbine Aircraft Services; Jens Hennig, General Aviation Manufacturers Association; Sandy and JoAnn Hill, National Association of Flight Instructors; Sean Lane, ASA Publishing; Jim Lauerman, Avemco; Stan Mackiewicz, National Air Transportation Association; Arlynn McMahon, Aero-Tech Incorporated; Tim McSwain, USAIG; Rusty Sachs, National Association of Flight Instructors; Roger Sharp, Cessna Pilot Centers; Jackie Spanitz, ASA; Howard Stoodley, Manassas Aviation Center; Michele Summers, Embry-Riddle Aeronautical University; and Max Trescott, SJFlight.

It is intended to be a living document that incorporates comments, suggestions, and ideas for best practices from GA instructors like you. Please direct comments and ideas for future iterations to:

susan.parson@faa.gov

Happy—and safe—flying!

Appendix 2
Flight Review Checklist

Appendix 2

This is a recommended flight review. Procedures may be added or removed at the issuing flight instructor's discretion, based on the individual candidate's needs, goals, and experience level.

Step 1
Preparation

The following is an example of an instructor checklist of questions to ask the pilot applicant taking the flight review.

Name _____ Telephone _____

Address _____

Certificates, ratings _____

Current now? ___ yes ___ no. If no, how long since current? _____

What type of flying do you typically do? _____

Last training? _____

How much flying time in last year? _____

Aircraft for test (make and model) _____

N number _____

Areas where training might be needed (weak areas) _____
_____

Goals/objectives for flight review (currency in aircraft, completion of *WINGS* phase, etc.) _____

Location of test (including time and date) _____

Class of airman medical certificate or valid U.S. driver's license
   (if applicable) _____

Aircraft—certificates, logbooks, and equipment _____

Logbook flight time records _____

Fee discussed with payment obligation _____

Part 91 review* _____
*(Candidate can complete FAA online Flight Review course found at **faasafety.gov**, bring the certificate of achievement with them to the flight review, and/or complete the written exercise as assigned by the flight instructor.)*

Cross-country flight plan assignment _____

Appendix 2

Step 2
Ground Review

- ☐ Regulatory review
- ☐ Cross-country flight plan review
- ☐ Weather briefing review; weather decision-making
- ☐ Risk management and personal minimums
- ☐ General aviation security issues
- ☐ Visual inspection of aircraft: airworthiness (inspect paperwork), weight and balance (CG within limits), airplane performance and limitations

Step 3
Flight Activities

Structure the flight portion as an out-and-back VFR cross-country (XC) with one leg to focus on XC procedures (including diversion and lost procedures) and the other leg to focus on airwork.

- ☐ Airmanship (aeronautical decision-making, systems knowledge, use of checklists, collision avoidance, avoidance of hazardous weather, proper use of airspace, communications and navigation)
- ☐ Takeoff (normal, cross-wind, short-field, soft-field)
- ☐ Steep turns
- ☐ Slow flight
- ☐ Stalls (power on, power off)
- ☐ Flight by reference to instruments (recovery from unusual attitudes, straight and level, turns to headings)
- ☐ Simulated emergency operations (emergency landing, equipment malfunction)
- ☐ Landings (normal, cross-wind, short-field, soft-field, go-arounds, simulated forced/emergency)
- ☐ Postflight procedures (after landing, parking, securing)

Step 4
Postflight Discussion

- ☐ Review knowledge skills (strengths, weaknesses)
- ☐ Review flight skills (strengths, weaknesses)
- ☐ Questions
- ☐ Discuss aeronautical health maintenance and improvement plan (personal minimums checklist, personal proficiency practice plan, training plan if desired)
- ☐ Logbook endorsement (if satisfactory completion ***only***)

Appendix 3
Developing Personal Minimums

Appendix 3

Federal Aviation Administration

Developing *Personal* Minimums

Think of personal minimums as the human factors equivalent of reserve fuel. Personal minimums should provide a solid safety buffer between:

- *Skills required* for the specific flight, and
- *Skills available* to you through your training, experience, currency, and proficiency.

Step 1 - Review Weather Minimums

Step 2 - Assess Weather Experience and Personal Comfort Level

Step 3 - Consider Winds and Performance

Step 4 - Assemble Baseline Values

Step 5 - Adjust for Specific Conditions

Step 6 - Stick to the Plan!

FAA Safety Briefing, March/April 2015, "Your Safety Reserve: Developing Your Personal Minimums" by Susan Parson.

Appendix 3

Step 1: Review definitions for VFR & IFR weather minimums.

Category	Ceiling		Visibility
VFR	greater than 3,000 AGL	and	greater than 5 miles
MVFR	1,000 to 3,000 AGL	and/or	3 to 5 miles
IFR	500 to 999 AGL	and/or	1 mile to less than 3 miles
LIFR	below 500 AGL	and/or	less than 1 mile

Step 2(a): Record certification, training, & recent experience.

CERTIFICATION LEVEL	
Certificate level (e.g., private, commercial, ATP)	
Ratings (e.g., instrument, multiengine)	
Endorsements (e.g., complex, HP, high altitude)	
TRAINING SUMMARY	
Flight review (e.g., certificate, rating, Wings)	
Instrument Proficiency Check	
Time since checkout in airplane 1	
Time since checkout in airplane 2	
EXPERIENCE	
Total flying time	
Years of flying experience	
RECENT EXPERIENCE (last 12 months)	
Hours	
Hours in this airplane (or identical model)	
Normal Landings	
Crosswind landings	
Night hours	
Night landings	
Hours flown in high density altitude	
Hours flown in mountainous terrain	
IFR hours	
IMC hours (actual conditions)	
Approaches (actual or simulated)	
Time with specific GPS navigator	
Time with specific autopilot	

Appendix 3

Step 2(b): Enter values for weather experience/ "comfort level."

Experience & "Comfort Level" Assessment Combined VFR & IFR					
Weather Condition		VFR	MVFR	IFR	LIFR
Ceiling					
	Day				
	Night				
Visibility					
	Day				
	Night				

Step 3(a): Enter values for experience/ comfort in turbulence.

Experience & "Comfort Level" Assessment Wind & Turbulence			
	SE	ME	Make/Model
Turbulence			
Surface wind speed			
Surface wind gusts			
Crosswind component			

Step 3(b): Enter values for performance.

Experience & "Comfort Level" Assessment Performance Factors			
	SE	ME	Make/Model
Performance			
Shortest runway			
Highest terrain			
Highest density altitude			

Appendix 3

Step 4: Assemble and evaluate baseline personal minimums

Baseline Personal Minimums					
Weather Condition		VFR	MVFR	IFR	LIFR
Ceiling					
	Day				
	Night				
Visibility					
	Day				
	Night				

	SE	ME	Make/Model	
Turbulence				
Surface wind speed				
Surface wind gusts				
Crosswind component				

	SE	ME	Make/Model	
Performance				
Shortest runway				
Highest terrain				
Highest density altitude				

Step 5: Adjust for specific Conditions

	If you are facing:		Adjust baseline personal minimums to:
Pilot	Illness, medication, stress, or fatigue; lack of currency (e.g., haven't flown for several weeks)	A d d	At Least 500 feet to ceiling
Aircraft	An unfamiliar airplane, or an aircraft with unfamiliar avionics/ equipment:		At least ½ mile to visibility
enVironment	Airports and airspace with different terrain or unfamiliar characteristics		At least 500 ft to runway length
External Pressures	"Must meet" deadlines, passenger pressures; etc.	S u b t r a c t	At least 5 knots from winds

Appendix 4

FAA Over-the-Counter (OTC) Medications Reference Guide

Appendix 4

Federal Aviation Administration

Over-the-Counter (OTC) Medications Reference Guide

What Over-the-Counter (OTC) medications can I take and still be safe to fly?

First, ask yourself "Do I have an underlying condition that makes me unsafe to fly?" Title 14 CFR 61.53 is the regulation, which prohibits fight with a known medical defciency [unless cleared by the FAA] and requires that you determine that you are fit to fly prior to each fight.

- ☐ Am I sick?
    - ☐ Am I having trouble clearing my ears at ground level?
    - ☐ Do I feel bad enough that I keep thinking about how I feel?
    - ☐ Are others asking me if I am ok?
    - ☐ Do I feel good enough to fly ONLY if I take medication?
    - ☐ Am I getting worse?

Next, current issues. Consider these issues before operating an aircraft:

- ☐ In the last fve days, have you taken or do you plan to take any medications before flying?
- ☐ If currently taking a medication only for symptom relief, would you be safe to fly without it?
- ☐ Do you have any other underlying health conditions?
    - Discuss these conditions with your AME or family physician to determine if you are safe to fly.
    - Specifcally ask about your ability "to operate machinery" (including any aircraft).
    - Discuss if the medication, OTC or otherwise, will pose a problem with the underlying condition or
    - Other health conditions and/or other medications that you are taking.

Appendix 4

When choosing an OTC medication:

#1. IDENTIFY the active ingredient(s).
Verify you have taken this medication in the past with no side effects.
Note: Single ingredient products are preferred over combination products (because it is easier to spot potentially hazardous ingredients).

#2. READ the label.
If there is a warning that it "May cause drowsiness" or if it advises the user to "be careful when driving a motor vehicle or operating machinery," then this medication is NOT safe for flying.

#3. READ carefully.
If this is the first time you are taking a new medication, wait at least five (5) dosage intervals and ensure that you suffer no adverse effects from it before flying while on the medication. (See the table below for the recommended observation period).

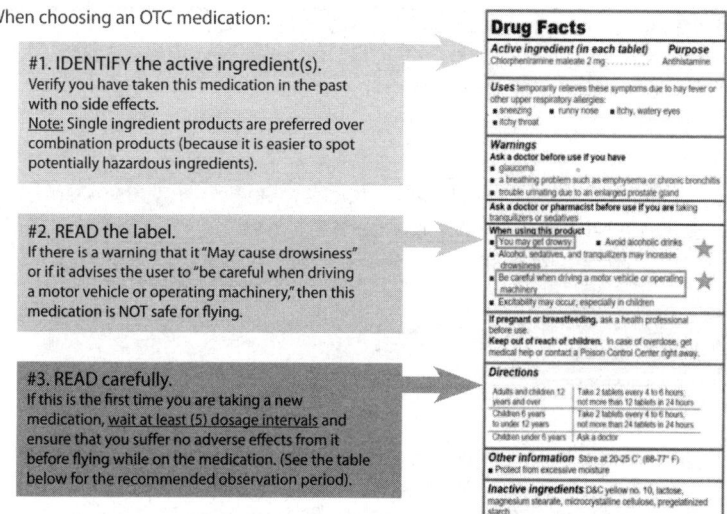

If you take any of the "NO GO" medications (listed below in the "Over-the-Counter (OTC) Medications Reference Table") or if you have previously had side effects from the medication, wait at least five (5) dosage intervals after the last dose before flying. See the examples below for the recommended grounding period after discontinuation of the medication).

  ***Caution:** Sedating antihistamine medications have a long half-life so wait time is **60 hours** for both **diphenhydraime (Benadryl)** and doxylamine (Unisom), 5 days for both chlorpheniramine and clemastine.

Dosage Interval Wait Time

Package Instructions	5 Times Dosage Interval	No Fly Time	Recommendation
Every 4-6 hours ^ (Up to 6 times daily)	X5	30 hours	Wait at least 30 hours before flying if taking a medication directed to take every 4-6 hours.
Every 8 hours (OR three times daily)	X5	40 hours	Wait at least 40 hours before flying if taking a medication directed to take every 8 hours.
Every 12 hours (OR twice daily)	X5	60 hours	Wait at least 60 hours before flying if taking a medication directed to take every 12 hours.

^ If there is a range, use the higher number

Appendix 4

Always follow 14 CFR 61.53. If it is not familiar to you, please review it. Not only is it a requirement, but it is for your safety and that of your passengers. When in doubt, safety first - do not fly.

- ☐ Never fly after taking a new medication for the frst time until at least 48 hours have passed and no side efects are noted.
- ☐ Do one more check of your condition before considering flying.
- ☐ Get well before considering return to fight status ... do not push it.
- ☐ OTC medications help reduce the symptoms of an illness, but do not cure it.
- ☐ Even though a medication has been determined to be safe for use by the Food and Drug Administration (FDA), this does not mean that the medication is compatible with flying or even driving.

Some medications are not recommended (see column "NO GO" on the table below):

- If you choose to fly on medication, be certain that it will not impair safety. Do not simply hope for the best.

NOTE: This list is not all-inclusive or intended to take the place of consultation(s) with your primary care physician and/or AME (aviation medical examiner). Remember, if you have signifcant underlying health conditions, it is recommended that the use of any medication be discussed with your physician PRIOR to taking the medication.

Appendix 4

Over-the-Counter (OTC) Medications Reference Table

Type of medication or symptoms	Commonly found in	Medication or active ingredient generally safe to fly **GO**	Avoid these medications or ingredients* **NO GO**	Rationale
Antihistamines[1]	Allergy products Cough/cold products Pain products	Non-sedating products: fexofenadine (Allegra) loratadine (Claritin)	Sedating products: brompheniramine (Dimetapp) cetirizine (Zyrtec) chlorpheniramine (Chlor-Trimeton) diphenhydramine (Benadryl) levocetirizine (Xyzal)	Histamines affect not only your allergies, but your sleep wake cycle. Sedating antihistamines can cause drowsiness, impaired thinking and judgement. [1] Sedating antihistamines are commonly found on autopsy in aircraft accidents. The wait times for these medications are longer than noted in the "Dosage Interval Wait Time" table due to their longer half-life. Consult your AME.
	Motion sickness		dimenhydrinate (Dramamine) meclizine (Antivert)	
	Sleep aid products	melatonin (not an antihistamine)	diphenhydramine (such as Zzzquil). Same ingredient in Benadryl Doxylamine (such as Unisom)	
Nasal steroid	Allergy products	azelastine (Astepro) fluticasone (Flonase) mometasone (Nasonex) triamcinolone (Nasacort)	None	
Nasal decongestants	Nasal congestion Sinus pressure Cough/cold products	oxymetazoline (Afrin) phenylephrine (Sudafed PE) pseudoephedrine (Sudafed) Less convenient, but safer, are the nasal salt water lavages: saline nasal sprays Neti-pots		Caution: Sudafed-like medications can speed up your heart rate; therefore, use caution if you have an underlying heart condition. Be very cautious of an extra cup of coffee or two when feeling sub-par. This has caused more than one pilot to end up in the emergency room for a racing heart rate.

Appendix 4

Type of medication or symptoms	Commonly found in	Medication or active ingredient generally safe to fly **GO**	Avoid these medications or ingredients* **NO GO**	Rationale
Cough	Cough/cold products	Coricidin (allowed if no chlorpheniramine) guaifenesin (found in Mucinex and Robitussin)	dextromethorphan (Delsym), also in Dayquil, and Mucinex Fast-Max Severe Congestion and Cough. Most "night-time" or "PM" medications contain a sedating antihistamine. - Coricidin HBP cough & cold (contains chlorpheniramine) - Nyquil (contains doxylamine)	Most cough medications are safe for flight. Use caution as combination products may contain sedating antihistamines. If the label states PM (for nighttime use) or DM (containing dextromethorphan), you should not fly while using these medications and for at least 5 dosage intervals after the last dose (see Dosage Interval Time table).
Aches and Pains	NSAIDs (nonsteroidal anti-inflammatory drugs) and analgesics	acetaminophen (Tylenol) aspirin (Bayer's) ibuprofen (Advil/Motrin) naproxen (Naprosyn)	Advil PM, Tylenol PM (Most "PM" medications contain diphenhydramine)	Most OTC pain meds are safe to fly as long as the underlying condition is acceptable. Caution: Some OTC meds are combined with a sedating antihistamine, which can cause drowsiness (see above for examples).
	Additional options for headaches	caffeine (commonly found in Excedrin)	Read the label.	
	Topical pain relief	lidocaine patch (Lidoderm) muscle rub capsaicin		Lidocaine: Caution with application. Avoid getting on hands or open wounds as this can drop blood pressure or absorb faster.
Opioid Antidote	Opioid antidote		naloxone (Narcan)[2]	[2] If medication is administered, DO NOT FLY until cleared by FAA.

Appendix 4

Type of medication or symptoms	Commonly found in	Medication or active ingredient generally safe to fly **GO**	Avoid these medications or ingredients* **NO GO**	Rationale
Gastrointestinal Illness: nausea, vomiting, diarrhea, constipation, laxatives	Anti-emetics anti-motility drugs	bismuth subsalicylate (Kaopectate, Pepto-Bismol)	loperamide (Imodium)[3]	GI illness can cause dehydration, cramps & pain with increase in altitude. [3] Loperamide should not be used during acute illness as it can cause dizziness. When taken daily for a chronic condition, may require a special issuance.
	Laxatives	Bulk forming (e.g. Benefiber) Osmotic (e.g. MiraLAX) Stool softener (e.g. Colace) Stimulant (e.g. Senna)	magnesium citrate	Use in recommended doses.
Gastrointestinal Illness: indigestion	Proton Pump Inhibitors (PPI)	esomeprazole (Nexium) lansoprazole (Prevacid) omeprazole (Prilosec) pantoprazole (Protonix) rabeprazole (Aciphex)	None	Be careful not to mask the underlying symptoms.
	H2 blockers	cimetidine (Tagamet) famotidine (Pepcid) nizatidine (Axid) rantidine (Zantac)	None	Be careful not to mask the underlying symptoms.
	Antacids	aluminum hydroxide (Maalox) calcium carbonate (Tums) magnesium hydroxide (Milk of Magnesia)	None	Be careful not to mask the underlying symptoms.
Urinary Tract Infections	Pain reliever	phenazopyridine (AZO standard)	oxybutynin (Oxytrol for Women)	Oxybutynin can cause sedation & Women) dizziness. Phenazopyridine is generally allowed after adequate ground trial to monitor for side effects. Symptoms should be resolved other than slight residual irritation.

Appendix 4

Type of medication or symptoms	Commonly found in	Medication or active ingredient generally safe to fly **GO**	Avoid these medications or ingredients* **NO GO**	Rationale
Skin Rash	Emollients Creams Lotions	almost all are allowed antifungal topical antipruritics corticosteroid topical		Ensure the underlying condition is not an issue with safe flight.
Eyes (Ophthalmic)	Products for Dry eyes Allergy/Itchy eyes Eye lubrication	olopatadine (Pataday) alcaftadine (Lastacaft) artificial tears	Eye ointment or gel during flight[4]	Temporary blurry vision may occur with use of eye drops. [4] Eye ointment or gels should not used in flight since the blurry vision may last for minutes.

Frequently Used OTC Medications   *These effectively can cause incapacitation (examples are not all-inclusive)

Appendix 4

Additional Resources

AAM-400 Medication Brochure
www.faa.gov/pilots/safety/pilotsafetybrochures

Over-the-Counter Medication
www.faa.gov/ame_guide/media/AME_OTC_medications.pdf

Allergy — Antihistamine & Immunotherapy Medication
www.faa.gov/ame_guide/media
/AllergyAntihistamineImmunotherapyMedication.pdf

Erectile Dysfunction Medication
www.faa.gov/ame_guide/pharm/ed

Hypertension Medication
www.faa.gov/ame_guide/pharm/antihyp

Diabetes Medications
Acceptable Combinations of Diabetic Medications
www.faa.gov/ame_guide/media/diabetesmeds_acceptablecomb.pdf

SSRI (antidepressant) Program
www.faa.gov/ame_guide/app_process/exam_tech/item47/amd
/antidepressants

Additional Medication Information in Guide for Aviation Medical Examiners
www.faa.gov/ame_guide/pharm

Do Not Issue (DNI) Do Not Fly (DNF)
www.faa.gov/ame_guide/pharm/dni_dnf

DNI—pilots should NOT take any of these medications or classes of medication and fly

DNF—pilots should NOT fly until these medications are stopped and a period of time has elapsed

Stay Informed with ASA's Online Resources

Reader resources and updates for the
Guide to the Flight Review for Pilots and Instructors:
asa2fly.com/oegbfr

Visit **asa2fly.com** for ASA's full selection of aviation books, training resources, apps, and pilot supplies.

asa2fly.com

Learn to Fly Blog—Where pilots and future pilots explore flight and flight training:
learntoflyblog.com

Follow, like, share.
- instagram.com/asa2fly
- facebook.com/asa2fly
- youtube.com/asa2fly
- linkedin.com/company/asa2fly